KT-417-368

TERRORISM
THE NEW WORLD WAR

TERRORISM
THE NEW WORLD WAR

**LLOYD PETTIFORD
& DAVID HARDING**

Capella

Published by Arcturus Publishing Limited

For Bookmart Limited
Registered number 2372865
Trading as Bookmart Limited
Desford Road, Enderby, Leicester LE19 4AD

This edition published 2003

©2003 Arcturus Publishing Limited

All rights reserved. No part of this publication may be
reproduced, stored in a retrieval system, or transmitted
in any form or by any means, electronic, mechanical,
photocopying, recording or otherwise, without written
permission or in accordance with the Copyright Act
1956 (as amended). Any person or persons who do any
unauthorised act in relation to this publication may be
liable to criminal prosecution and civil claims for damages.

British Library Cataloguing-in-Publication Data: a catalogue
record for this book is available from the British Library

Jacket design by Alex Ingr

Arcturus Publishing Limited
26/27 Bickels Yard, 151–153 Bermondsey Street,
London SE1 3HA

ISBN 1-84193-154-3

Printed in Denmark

CONTENTS

FOREWORD

WHO WAS RICHARD? He wasn't my best friend but I know that to many people he was. Richard was the sort of person that everyone liked. There didn't seem to be anything not to like. He worked too hard, but that's not much of a fault. If you ever really needed someone to listen, he was a good listener. Like many men, it seemed to me that it took him until his 30s to truly grow up, but by the last time I saw him he was truly grown up. Love, life and work were in perspective. Given the content of this book and the tense I have used you have probably already guessed; Richard was born in 1969 and died on 11 September 2001. However many times I read these words, it doesn't get any easier.

How am I, how are his other friends and family, and how are you to make sense of his death? Of course in one way, there is no answer. His death, at the hands of terrorists, was senseless, a waste; the positive impact he had on those who knew him a small, if important, consolation now. However, even according to the advice that one ought to know one's enemy, terrorism deserves more thought than some commentators and politicians have recently given it. Terrorism is unlikely to be eradicated through bombing it into submission, any more than it will be overcome through ignoring it. This book emerges from a genuine – and alas personal – concern with combating terrorism. Although for the most part it seeks to do this by providing the reader with information with which s/he can make up his/her own mind it is underwritten by a conviction that since violence breeds violence we should avoid fighting terror with terror and instead seek its deeper causes and look for more sophisticated solutions than unnecessarily killing innocent people. Jus ex injuria non oritur – rights do not arise from wrongs.

Lloyd Pettiford, April 2002

INTRODUCTION
IS THIS THE UNCOMFORTABLE TRUTH?

'America is a complex country which, in a childlike way, is only able to deal with certain truths ... We like them simple and, if necessary, we'll have them distorted.'

David Puttnam

AS A STARTING POINT, let us consider 11 September 2001. Could no one have seen this coming? Could nothing have stopped it? Of course airport security could have been tighter, but would a different outrage not have happened somewhere else if this one had been stopped? There has also been some speculation that some people knew it was going to happen. A US Senate report published around the time of the first anniversary of the September 11 attacks found that some members of the intelligence services were warning that an attack was imminent but these warnings were not heeded. Perhaps, indeed, George W Bush and others had some warning that something was going to happen sometime, somewhere. But it seems more likely that there was a general idea that something was going to happen, rather than anyone having knowledge of specifics that they then failed to do anything about. Taking this last point a stage further, there has even been speculation, notably in France and in the Arab world, that it was all a set up; perpetrated by the United States government or with US consent to justify repression abroad and allowing a heightened moral consensus at home – less tolerant and more fervently patriotic. This is not an argument (that the US government would justify mass slaughter in order to justify mass slaughter) that we accept, though it is regrettably a pertinent question as to why such a suggestion would ever gain currency at all. It may be worth thinking about, although it is also worth remembering that where terrorist actions take place, conspiracy theories are never very far behind.

The point to make is not so much about whether anyone could have physically prevented it happening, but more to say that some people *did* see it coming. Not everyone, of course, and the specifics were a shock and a tragedy for the vast majority. But, people may be surprised to know that the impending disaster had more or less been documented in black and white. For instance Nicholas Guyatt's *Another American Century*, published in 2000 and obviously before '9/11', is remarkably explicit. Guyatt argues first that 'many people around the world are frustrated by the complacency and impenetrability of the US and that the apparent absence of political solutions to this (such as a genuinely multilateral and independent United Nations) is likely to drive many towards radical and extreme measures'. A consequence, he goes on to argue, is that there are 'large and dangerous pockets of resentment towards the US around the world, grounded not in fundamentalism or insanity but in a real perception of the imbalance of power, and a real frustration at the impotence of political means of change.' (pp.152–3).

But beyond these general warnings, Guyatt notes the tendency of the US to lash out with violence rather than seeking to understand the political motivations of terrorism. He suggests that this refusal to see events such as the attempted bombing of the World Trade Center in 1993 as *political* events 'will ultimately encourage a small minority to express their grievances in horrific ways... by attacking American interests abroad and even targeting cities within the US.' It is tragic surely that a little-known author can see with more clarity than the US President that 'as long as the US remains insulated from the effects of its actions it will have little sense of the true desperation they produce in others; and of the terrible predicament of those – in Iraq, or Sudan or Palestinian territories – who can find meaning and promise in an act of recklessness and destruction.' (pp.155–6)

These are by no means isolated claims of Guyatt's book but a theme of his well documented and convincing argument which he goes back to time and again. So, more concretely, what is his argument and how does he make it? Well, we should first note that several commentators have pointed out the folly of various foreign policy endeavours on the part of the United States throughout history. Even proud Americans have termed it 'arrogant and cruel' (Hertsgaard, 2002) but usually such 'folly', 'arrogance' and 'cruelty' can be dismissed or explained away on the grounds that it happened in the past and that given the chance to repent the United States surely would. An accompanying argument has also been put forward that in the climate of the Cold War and the struggle against the evils of communism the United States had frequently (and regrettably) to side with some unseemly characters as the lesser of evils. Thus it was that the United States was among those supporting Saddam Hussein as a stabilizing force within Iraq against Shia Muslims and Kurdish nationalists and regionally against the Ayatollahs and Shia Iran. Thus it was that the United States has sided with brutal military dictatorships in places such as El Salvador and Indonesia. Thus it was that the United States helped found the so-called 'University of Terrorism', along with one Osama bin Laden in Afghanistan, as the Mujahaddin fought the Soviet Union.

So, whilst some of this may be regrettable or shocking, as suggested above the counter-argument is often that it was necessary in the struggle against communism, and that things are different now and the United States is now committed to good things like peace and democracy and free to bring the world salvation, showering it with beneficence and kindness. Alas, it is precisely this argument that Guyatt is able to convincingly knock down. He argues that while the United States has indeed announced the post-Cold War era as a new one of international cooperation, in actuality it has been committed to unilateral action rather than the multilateralism of genuine international cooperation. He argues that in Somalia, Iraq and Kosovo this determination to use overwhelming force and to do things its own way cost thousands upon thousands of innocent lives. Furthermore, when the United States has not wanted to act – as in Rwanda – its desire nonetheless to control the situation has led to it effectively stifling genuine multilateral efforts and resulting in many more thousands of deaths.

In this way we can see that the United States, in the post Cold War era as well as in that struggle against communism itself, has been responsible for the over-control of global politics – rather than genuine multilateralism – and in this way has really been responsible for the deaths of countless thousands. For these reasons, Guyatt argues that the world community is thus unable to act without US permission, limiting what can be done, but also that US policies are creating resentment, and a feeling among certain groups that their only recourse is to lash out with acts of unspeakable terror.

So the warnings were surely there that US policy was creating the monster it feared. But regrettably the US chose not to heed those warnings and has continued to act unilaterally post '9/11'. In a strangely non-conformist way – for the Western media – the British newspaper the *Daily Mirror* pointed out in its edition of 4 July 2002 ('Mourn on the 4th of July') that since 11 September the US air campaign over Afghanistan had killed twice as many people as the 11 September attack itself. These figures are contentious only because no exact number can be arrived at and any final number is reliant on reports from remote areas of Afghanistan. But it is clear that many people died because of the bombing and somewhere close to the number that were killed on 11 September in the United States. Such a continuing disregard by the US for the lives of non-Americans seems certain to keep it regarded by many as the world's biggest terrorist and to create more and more people prepared to commit outrages against it as their only means of expression in a world without political choice. A world where the US (and its capitalist offspring) enforces ever more cultural, social and economic conformity. Is this the uncomfortable truth?

1 REMARKS ON TERROR

Nothing is easier to denounce than the evil doer;
Nothing is more difficult than to understand him.

Fyodor Dostoevsky

To try and explain and understand terrorism is not to justify
terrorism. But if you don't try to explain anything, you will never
learn anything.

Howard Zinn, 2002, p.17.

THE GRIEF OR TRAGEDY which accompanies a terrorist attack can lead to a rather uni-dimensional view of terrorism. For those personally affected by the loss of loved ones and friends this uni-dimensionality focuses on their loss, and not, we suspect, on blood-lust and revenge. But for those not directly linked to events, the feeling is perhaps entirely understandable that someone ought to be held accountable and that someone be made to pay. This feeling is accentuated by a feeling of power-lessness. Like the victims of many types of crime, there is a feeling of profound disempowerment at having no way of righting the wrong suffered. But despite the powerful and simple emotions that can overcome people at times of personal, national or global tragedy the reality of terror is, alas, much more complicated: 'Terrorism is a complex problem: Its origins are diverse; and so are those who engage in it.' (Reich, 1990, p1). This book is an attempt to explore this complexity in the belief that complex problems rarely have simple answers.

Before moving to discuss issues of what actually constitutes terrorism, it should be stressed that the attempt here is not to condone the actions of the terrorist nor to provide simply a 'bar-room philosophy' course in ethics and violence. Though the underlying conviction of the authors is that violence is wrong, we find enough examples through history of those who have inspired us by fighting for what they believed in that we cannot make this argument unqualified. Fascism, for instance, had to be fought. Dictatorships sometimes get removed by violence when nothing else would work – think of Ceaucescu and Somoza. So, as mentioned above, information and a context within which to think about it is what we are aiming at. In a world of entrenched opinion and knee-jerk reaction, thinking is essential.

Accordingly, one of the first functions of this book is to provide a comprehensive guide to terrorism with clear accounts of historical terror, the evolution and emergence of the term, biographies of terrorist groups and details of individual terrorist acts and individual terrorists. In selecting material for these sections we are guided by the idea that terrorism can be defined as violence against (innocent) civilians. In doing so, we seek to escape from any personal feelings about recent events and to combine this with an argument that whether something constitutes terror or not has often been a judgment of history. In this way we hope that the book is able to dispel any simplistic notion of terrorism, without spreading the term so widely as to include sabotage, intimidation and all violence more generally.

Here we realize problems can emerge. Is a politician an inno-cent civilian? The unhelpful answer is almost certainly 'not always'. There is a long history of people providing justification for killing leaders; as Spanish Jesuit scholar Juan de Mariana once put it 'if in no other way it is possible to save the fatherland, the prince should be killed by the sword as a public enemy.' (in Combs, 1997, p.23). Do rich people benefiting from a corrupt system or profiting from others' misery deserve to qualify as innocent? Despite such problems in defining 'innocent' our focus remains on people who were broadly speaking in the wrong place at the wrong time rather than explicit and defined targets.

In looking at other histories of terrorism it is interesting to see how differently the problem is approached. Our definition above is an effort to impose some limits on the material covered, whilst at the same time allowing us to see beyond political par-tiality. There is an easy tendency to equate terrorism with acts of violence done by other people we don't like against people we do, whilst violence done by people we do like, against those we don't justifies for them the title of freedom fighter. But if we act as judge and jury as to what constitutes terror we may miss the impact of terror committed in our names. This is why we con-centrate on civilian deaths and the 'end of innocents'. Other definitions elaborate such an idea but retain a similar core. Combs argues that terrorism is 'a synthesis of war and theater, a dramatization of the most proscribed kind of violence – that which is perpetrated on innocent victims – played before an audience in the hope of creating a mood of fear, for political pur-poses.' (1997, p. 8). But we restrict our definition because some terror we would argue is covert; that it seeks to terrorize without publicity – particularly state terror.

In doing so we must be careful also to distinguish between

deliberate acts and accidents. The number killed in the World Trade Center in 2001 was roughly equivalent to the numbers killed in the immediate aftermath of the Bhopal tragedy in India in 1984 when a chemical leak occurred at a Union Carbide factory (although deaths attributed to that accident, as well as birth defects, continue to increase to this day, with numbers of dead estimated at around 20,000 in total). If it were possible to prove that these deaths were caused by Union Carbide ought that not to be described as 'corporate terror'? Should a war on capitalism have occurred as a result? The answer is of course, and evidence strongly suggests this to be the case, that responsibility here is in the sense of negligence. Somebody or some people are undoubtedly felt responsible for the Bhopal disaster – banners displayed at the Bhopal memorial leave no doubt as to the feelings of locals on this point – but they did not set out with the aim of killing people. Terrorism has to be a deliberate strategy to count as such.

The preceding paragraphs have sought to establish that terrorism cannot simply be equated with anything that kills or is bad. Similarly we cannot simply equate the terrorist him or herself with being bad people. A psychological study of terrorism starts off with the question, what enables 'human beings to carry out acts that contravene the deepest moral precepts that ordinarily contain them?' (Reich, 1990, p1). A good question, but it surely does not only apply to terrorism. It also applies to war, and as we have intimated above most people would not condemn all wars in the same way they would condemn terrorism. Sometimes it appears there are good reasons to fight for what we believe in and, if you talk to people who have fought in such a war, this sometimes requires acts which contravene their deepest moral precepts.

Herein lies one of the most uncomfortable truths. Terrorists commit acts of unspeakable barbarity which we have not the slightest idea how to comprehend, but terrorists are rarely complete madmen engaged in random and wanton violence. From the Maoist guerrilla war of Sendero Luminoso in Peru, to the political struggle of the IRA to the jihad or holy war, there is usually a reasoning, calculating person directing the killing. We must condemn the acts these people commit as barbaric but in even beginning to combat them we must comprehend how the acts are justified by those who commit them as acts of war or of political or religious or nationalist struggle. Moreover, if we look into history, or even the personal histories of terrorists we do not always find simply evil: we find perceived injustice – we find, in other words, reasons. Where there are reasons we have to understand as well as just attack because if we do not we are simply encouraging a downward spiral of violence. Perhaps the conditions which created today's terrorist will create others tomorrow unless we change them.

Faced with terrorist outrage, this urging to understanding may seem like so much liberal wishy-washy nonsense. But it is important. As we shall see in the pages to come, terrorism has a long history of thought and practice, even in its modern form going back over 200 years. When we think about terrorism in history, even before it was called such, we can start to separate ourselves from individual acts of violence and acquire much-needed perspective as a result. We hear histories of people who have faced up to injustice and we admire what they have done, even though it may have included violent acts. We might regard these people as heroes, though at the time they were considered as villains (wanted dead or alive) or traitors; the terrorists of their time.

For example, Robin Hood (a myth for sure) and US revolutionaries are examples of people who in their day would have been regarded – using today's terminology – as terrorists. (Indeed Mullah Omar was initially regarded in Afghanistan as a Robin Hood type figure in freeing women and men from the random barbarity of warlords). Folklore has defined Robin, and history the US revolutionaries more kindly, however, than Mullah Omar is regarded today. History argues that what they did was legitimate given the circumstances they faced. History has forgotten those who denounced their acts. But folklore – and history – are almost certainly too kind. Robin Hood struck fear into the hearts of good, though admittedly rich, people. US revolutionary armies not only sought to overthrow the existing system, but in order to do so forced conscription and then forced people to fight and shoot deserters. Surely by today's standards this kind of behaviour is terrorist?

Anyone hijacking planes, stealing people's cash and belongings and then distributing it in the Favelas of Rio would possibly not be presented by the world's press as a hero today but as a dangerous menace with no respect for private property. And as for anyone who suggested that the United States presented an unjust system of government which ought to be overthrown by violent revolt, we can surely doubt they would be popularly received and acclaimed. History gives perspective and allows us to understand terrorism better. From the French Resistance to Nelson Mandela history allows the relatively uncontroversial rehabilitation and re-labeling of terrorism. Concentrating on the deliberate killing of innocent civilians, by whomever and whenever, allows us to be clear about what is terrorism without becoming confused by political justifications.

If we look at the French Revolution (the foundation of the

modern French state) whose bloody course has been reflected in that nation's stirring anthem, we see that terror was clearly an explicit tactic of the revolutionaries. At the time, victims of that terror were guilty, but from the perspective of today the victims could in some way be considered innocent. However, they were legitimate targets of those who wanted change. It is, alas, another facet of the problem that the victims of terrorism are rarely entirely innocent to those who kill them. Even when they are innocent they can still be considered unimportant by-products of the struggle. Terrorism tends to dehumanize the enemy; thus the terrible acts committed by the government of El Salvador, most notably in the 1970s and 1980s, supported by the United States, reduced a vast multitude of journalists, lawyers, teachers, students, intellectuals and priests to 'leftists' – a faceless enemy against whom all methods of terror were thus justified.

To sum up this introduction, we are not arguing that 'it is all relative' and that we cannot make judgments between what is good and bad. However, in taking a historical and broad view of terrorism, we can discover that judgments are often very selective. In short the 'war against terrorism' should not become a blanket acceptance of all 'we' do and a blanket condemnation of dissent. It should not become a case of being either for or against. Combating terrorism is in part about creating a world where the idea of terrorism becomes meaningless.

ABOUT THIS BOOK

So, if you were expecting to pick up this book and to read about Osama Bin Laden, do read on. Terror is terror and if someone is capable of encouraging planes to be flown into buildings then any amount of reflection on reasons is not going to make that right. But if you were expecting the history of terrorism to be an easily traceable one of evil and its perpetual struggle with good, you may be in for a surprise. A couple of phrases might get us off on the right foot in this regard; a cautious foot where good and evil are never as clear cut as they seem and where the truth – to echo Margaret Thatcher – is a very difficult concept. The first is this:

> *One person's terrorist is another*
> *person's freedom fighter*

How many people can claim to be genuinely pacifist? How many of your friends would your government have to kill before you became violent and sought to 'fight back'? Or how many years of grinding poverty and repression before you tried to change the system? And if you did you'd surely expect the label 'freedom fighter' rather than terrorist. George Kennan, in writing about the rise in terrorist violence in Russia in the late 19th century sums things up. 'Wrong a man, deny him all redress, exile him if he complains, gag him if he cries out, strike him in the face if he struggles, and at the last he will stab and throw bombs.' (in Combs, p.29). Of course, you think it most unlikely that you live in a place where political and economic freedom are likely to be attacked in these ways, but very few of us are not potential terrorists in this sense. Though such a scenario is unlikely, would you put up with whatever was thrown at you? If the Soviet Union had won the Cold War would you be accepting the consequences or would you fight back? You probably like to think you'd fight back; Tass and Pravda would then have you on the most wanted terrorist list! The second key phrase is this:

History tends to get written by
the winners and the powerful

It is amazing how easily history can get rewritten (and interpreted differently) and how easily governments use an airbrush to erase what they don't want people to see. We cannot doubt that history would be different in textbooks if the Soviet Union had triumphed in the Cold War, and so we should also not doubt that the history we are actually told is the history of winners too. History is not neutral and impartial, alas: if al-Qaeda won the 'War against Terrorism' would the history they taught still regard the attack on the World Trade Center as the monstrosity we know it to be? Probably not. It might instead be considered a glorious beginning, or a regrettable but 'necessary' act? But these changes in history would not alter the facts of the act itself, and its wrongness. History is about interpretation. We can believe in truth and justice, but experience suggests it is not always victorious.

This is not to say that we cannot make judgements. This is not to say that we cannot write or talk about terrorism as something with real meaning. But the two phrases above make it clear that the person who is really interested in terrorism needs an open mind, a very open mind, at the outset. A journey through the history of terrorism is not as simple as you might think and, on the part of governments and terrorists alike, filled with hypocrisy and tragedy. Lies are told in the name of truth. Atrocities are committed in the name of peace. Fear instilled in the name of freedom. Anything, apparently, can be justified in the name of justice.

In order to get a handle on some of these 'slogans' and in an effort to think beyond our gut responses to terror, this book begins with a look at terrorism in historical perspective. This is important. Our instincts about right and wrong mean that the idea is widely discussed and little understood. The fact that psychologists and political scientists are able to offer us so little by way of explaining the phenomenon seems to suggest that terrorism is a recent phenomenon. However, the philosophical and theological debate over the rightness of killing political opponents stems back for thousands of years, at least to the great ancient Greek philosophers Plato and Aristotle. This important contextualization suggests to us an important conclusion: demands cannot be bombed out of existence any more than they can be achieved by bombs. A future free of terrorism has to be one based on justice rather than privilege, in which demands are discussed and negotiated and where genuine grievances are addressed. Where, first and foremost, genuine political expression is possible.

This historical structure having been established the reader will be aware of enough caveats about the problems of definition in the case of terrorism that the remaining chapters should inform but also raise questions. The reader is not asked to abandon their convictions, and in no case to condone violence and the taking of innocent lives. However, the complexity of the problem should become apparent. That the solution to terror does not involve killing a few madmen should also become apparent; whilst this might be possible in a few cases, where the terror is based on a fundamental political, national or religious sense of injustice or powerlessness, violence will tend to breed violence.

The main chapters will concentrate on different facets of the problem. First a range of terrorist groups will be examined. Al-

Qaeda will spring to many minds of course at this time, but from white supremacists in the US to the IRA, Italian Red Brigade, Corsican Liberation movement and so on, there are a great many other groups to look at. It will become apparent that terrorism is not unidimensional in any sense. There are a variety of different types of cause to which the terrorist is committed. There are also a variety of different methods employed whatever their cause. To help the book be comprehensive, without being dull, we will mention through one line entries smaller groups who may have had a marginal impact such as the Scottish National Liberation Army.

We will also look at state terror. Whilst not normally included in a definition of terrorism, it is important to recognize the phenomenon. The fact that state terror is not usually referred to as terrorism shows that those with power can choose who to regard as terrorists. This chapter will cover not just state-sponsored terrorism (such as that which has been associated with Libya) but also terror as an explicit tactic of the state, as in for instance Stalin's Soviet Union, Argentina in the 1970s and early 1980s, Pinochet's Chile, modern day Colombia and in both Turkey and Iraq against the Kurdish peoples. The state is clever, and is unlikely to admit its actions to be terrorist (shrouded in the cloak of legitimacy as they are), but an examination of the behaviour of certain states suggests the use of violence as a political tactic and implies the death of many civilians.

Before drawing conclusions, a further chapter will look at the nature of possible future terrorism. What is a 'war on terrorism' likely to mean? What about the possibility of biological terrorism or 'rogue states' acquiring weapons of mass destruction? What may be the role of ecological terrorism or possible business involvement in seeking to control safe investment environments. Violence has increasingly been employed against particular ethnic groups within countries and against places where gay men are known to gather for instance. Having set up the fluid terms of possible argument over ·exactly what terrorism is, the book will largely describe events rather than seeking a political judgment. Keeping the idea in mind of 'civilians as victims' should allow this to be possible and leads to the 'obvious' conclusion that terrorism is always wrong and should not be supported whether the victims are Americans, Afghans, Bosnian-Serbs, Irish, Algerian or whatever. Terrorism is never justifiable, although it is always justified by someone and according to some political agenda. The war against terrorism looks a good deal more complicated than George W. Bush would have us believe.

2 A HISTORY OF TERRORISM

AT THE RISK of overdoing an already stated theme of this book, and in case you decided to miss the introduction, what is and is not terrorism can frequently come down to moral and/or historical judgement. That is why the title of this chapter is 'A History of Terrorism' and not 'The History of Terrorism'. Using the idea of 'A History' seeks to affirm that this is only one attempt to draw the boundaries of a phenomenon and not a dangerous/difficult moral judgment on where all the good and evil is in the world. Only a fool, at least in the human realm, would feel themselves equipped to pronounce ultimate judgment on that one, although it is significant that so many people nowadays actually do feel themselves qualified to talk with absolute certainty about their moral and other positions. As much as possible therefore, we ask the reader to approach the following material not with righteous indignation at everything which does not automatically strike a chord with their own sentiments, but with an open and questioning attitude secure only in the knowledge of human fallibility.

Beyond such a request, the following ought also to be proceeded by what at least some recent events have tended to demonstrate; that this is a history with many unexpected turns along the way and a history which has been in no sense uniform and unchanging. Where this history goes next is the subject of some speculation in later chapters but our conclusions in this regard ought only to be regarded as tentative. Though today George W. Bush may constantly re-emphasize the threat from terror, whilst others queue up to stand at his shoulder in the war against it, it is only a decade, after all, since Lawrence Howard's academic edited text on terrorism opened up with the statement that 'Terrorism, abhorrent as it is, is largely a symbolic threat to America.' (Howard, 1992, p.1). And whilst one might claim that, set alongside killers like obesity, AIDS, smoking, hand-gun use and traffic accidents, the threat actually is still relatively small, regrettably the only symbolic thing about 11 September was the choice of targets. If this can be read as a warning that this book – like Howard's – may soon be out of date, it ought also to suggest a need for flexibility rather than dogma in our thinking on, and responses to, terrorism.

MAY THE FORCE BE WITH YOU

So, to begin: A long time ago in a galaxy far, far away... the reason for starting with these well-known words is that if the 'futuristic' Star Wars really was a long time ago, say 10,000 years, we really ought to begin a history of terrorism with George Lucas' expanding series. If this seems odd, it can also serve a purpose. We ought to remind ourselves that Luke Skywalker, Han Solo, Princess Leah and even those fuzzy little Ewoks were undoubtedly terrorists, although of course the story is not told in that way. Skywalker and his alliance friends called themselves 'freedom fighters' and 'rebels' and characterize the Empire as the 'dark side' but really the Imperial forces were simply the pow-erful (and corrupt) trying to control their system of government.

The powerful and corrupt have a habit of labelling others as terrorists, as we shall see, whilst justifying their own violence in terms of essential control and protecting freedom. The parallels with today are obvious to some (Blum, 2001). It is almost embarrassing to hear some commentators today try to draw distinctions between terrorism and counter-terrorism or to justify what is done by 'their' people whilst condemning what is done by others. But Star Wars shows just how easy it is to set up the story to favor the terrorist.

Star Wars' 'feel-good factor' is much diminished if we tell a different story and instead characterize the Empire's stormtroopers as counter-insurgency forces engaged in their own war on terror. As the audience of Star Wars, *because of the way the story is told*, we are convinced of where to draw the dividing line between good and evil and we eagerly support the 'rebels' seeking to overthrow the unjust system of government; as the 'Death Star' is destroyed we do not gasp in horror at the loss of life implied in this action but instead rejoice at the bravery of Skywalker and justify his actions in terms of the many lives subsequently saved by it. The (uncomfortable) point that must be acknowledged – even if not accepted as valid - is that those who use violence to rid themselves of what they perceive as injustice in today's world (those who we might name 'terrorist') are just as convinced and sure that they sit firmly on the side of the good – even if they are wrong.

Rarely is violence random, but instead justified in the name of the greater good; even if we rightly reject categorically this rationale across the board, we have to accept that it is a rationale. We must attack the rationale (the reasons); we cannot eliminate the threat by eliminating individuals. Star Wars' heroes would have stopped fighting if the Empire ceased to be evil! But whilst it continued to be evil it would encourage more and more to take up arms against it even if Skywalker and Leah had themselves been killed. In other words, clampdown and repression encourage more terrorists.

Of course, Star Wars is only a film: it does, however encapsulate fully some of the dilemmas of defining and discussing terrorism. We might say that the violence of Skywalker and his friends is scant compared to that of the Empire and that this justifies it. But the Empire might make the same defence that the United States can and does; in the Gulf War, Kosovo and Afghanistan – in just the last decade or so – standing up to the rebels can be a messy business and regrettably takes innocent lives. Reading this, of course, you might say 'but the USA had to take action in bombing Iraq, Serbia and Afghanistan' and this is very different from destroying Alderan. You might argue that the conniving and evil of the Emperor were such that the rebel alliance was justified. But how much violence must be suffered here and now – in the real world – before someone can legitimately use violence? This is a rhetorical but important question, especially in the context of a hugely unequal world where 'violence' is lived every day by millions in the context of grinding poverty and the desperate scramble for existence on the scrap heap, in the sweatshop, in the gang and on the streets.

And before we move on to look further at that real world, it is worth mentioning that loveable rogue Han Solo. Reluctantly he helps Skywalker and the alliance, and his heroism wins us over, but at heart he is nothing but a common criminal. And since terrorists commit criminal acts the distinction is not always easy or clear-cut between terrorist, hero and criminal. So too in the history of terrorism this is a difficult distinction to hold on to and terrorists in the 19th century sometimes had ideas about the potential for social change of such anarchic criminal elements. Profit here is probably the key, with terrorists not acting out of personal greed. But even then it is not simple; those who sold crack cocaine in Los Angeles to finance the Contra rebels' terrorist activities against the government of Nicaragua in the 1980s probably did not have decimation of sections of the black community via crack nor profit as their motivations, but got both.

In fact, the real history of terrorism is no less awkward or difficult to fathom than the counter-intuitive idea that the good guys are, in fact, the terrorists in Star Wars. There is always a moral justification provided for terrorism regardless of moral authority. Yasser Arafat would certainly not regard Luke Skywalker as a terrorist. As he said to the 1974 UN General Assembly (Arafat, not Skywalker):

The difference between the revolutionary and the terrorist lies in the reason for which each fights. For whoever stands by a just cause and fights for the freedom and liberation of his land from the invaders, the settlers and the colonialists cannot possibly be called terrorists.

Yasser Arafat , cited in Hoffman, 1998, p.26.

The trouble is I might want to liberate my land from foreign influence, or liberate it from communism, or imperialism, or Jews. How can we be certain of what a just cause is? Depending on personal position or prejudice a just cause might be capitalism or socialism or Islam or less government interference or opposition to abortion or homophobia. And so on and so forth. And does a just cause justify anything?

The foregoing is not pretending to provide clear-cut answers, but to emphasize that what follows, though presented chronologically, does not and cannot provide us with a nice linear narrative, taking the reader from a clearly defined point A to a clearly defined point B in which we can put all the 'baddies' on one side and all the 'goodies' on another. Like the classic 'western' cowboy and Indian picture reality is rarely that simply and history offers a different perspective. The history of terrorism; a history of terrorism: any history of terrorism is a messy, moral maze. Resolving its contradictions today will not be simple, however simply they are stated by simple people. That said, we can begin to look at the historical origins of modern terror.

THE FRENCH REVOLUTION AND BEFORE

Leaving aside the fantasy world of Star Wars, the history of terrorism really does start a long time ago. Certainly the question of whether it is justifiable to kill a political opponent has been debated by philosophers and theologians for over 2000 years. Both Plato and Aristotle considered tyranny as a perversion, for instance, and Plato (c429–347 BC) in his *Republic* and more fully Aristotle (384–322 BC) in *Politics* discuss the question and morality of tyrannicide (the killing of a despotic or evil ruler).

There is then a long history, stemming from these Greek philosophers, of regarding tyrants as 'inviting' death or violent overthrow; of getting their just deserts in other words. Acts of political killing are thus glorified in the works of poets and playwrights from Harmodios and Aristogeiton onwards. Cicero notes in *De Officiis* that tyrants normally came to a violent end and that Romans celebrated this. Terrorism 'from below' (of the oppressed and downtrodden) has thus appeared from time immemorial for political and social reasons.

From the earliest times, terrorism has also been particularly associated with religious protest. One of the earliest examples of such a group was called the Sicarii, who were a highly organized religious sect active in the Zealot – anti-Roman – struggle in Palestine (AD 66–73); although to revisit one of the points made above, it can certainly be doubted whether this group was actually a terrorist organization or simply a group of violent criminals using religious frenzy as a screen for their activities. A more famous group, at least by name – and also a political/religious mix – were the Assassins. Suppressed by the Mongols in the 13th century, their leaders realized that they were too small to confront an enemy in battle, but by the selective use of terror they were able to maintain their religious autonomy through fear. (see Laqueur, 1987).

Considering the current horror at religiously motivated 'Islamic' terrorism, it is worth noting how many Christians throughout history have considered it their sacred duty to rid themselves violently of those in their way or those not following the 'correct' path. Some of the writings of Thomas Aquinas fall into this genre, though at the level of inspiration rather than practical example. Mediaeval writers chose examples from the Bible and Greeks and Romans to show that those who could not be trusted to use power responsibly should not be obeyed. Following this idea, Colonel Edward Saxby (publishing anonymously under the name William Allen) wrote a paper called 'Killing No Murder'. Saxby, a Leveller who aimed his paper at Oliver Cromwell, was executed, but his paper was given new life in translation (1793) during the French Revolution.

Indeed, despite the philosophical journey that can alert us to an ongoing debate about the morality of political violence throughout history, it is really with the French Revolution and the Jacobin Reign of Terror (1792–94) that we can, and should, date the beginnings of the modern use of the word 'terrorism', thus associating the phenomenon clearly from the start with the abuse of office and power, rather than attempts to overthrow it. We can certainly consider this to be terrorism in the sense that it was a deliberate strategy. The revolutionary leader Robespierre was able to argue that terror was 'nothing but justice, severe and inflexible' and that 'it is therefore an emanation of virtue' and vital for forging a new society. (Hoffman, 1998, pp.16–17).

The dating of modern terrorism to the late 18th century is almost convention, reflecting particular social, economic and political developments and that the word then came into use after this point. In other words revolutionary struggles of the time, the emergence of new economic forces and a developing discourse of (human) rights meant that it was time to give a name to terror. Though violence and injustice had been a common feature of (often monarchical and hierarchical) societies previously, a word was now needed for a particular form of horrible violence. Even so, we should remember that before this time torture, for instance, had been regarded as a standard (and not barbaric) practice and that violence and repression were common features of many societies. We might just as well, therefore, label the Spanish Inquisition as terrorism or peasant revolts as terrorism and some other surprising examples.

Though not called such now, US revolutionaries were undoubtedly terrorists; whatever inspiration they may subsequently have provided they did not, in the beginning, represent the views of more than a fraction (perhaps a third) of the population, although to be sure many were not pro-British either. The revolutionaries engaged in forced conscription, they shot deserters and they rebelled against the established authority of the time with violence; this surely makes them terrorists by today's standards. The British were quick to label them terrorists at the time. 'Shall a people that fifteen years ago was the terror of the world now stoop so low as to tell its ancient inveterate enemy, "Take all we have only give us peace?",' said the British Prime Minister William Pitt of the Americans and French in his last ever speech in Parliament. But, of course the victors get to write history: terrorism is not a word often associated with the independence of 1776. One person's terrorist really is another's freedom fighter!

Part of our problem in looking back is that in the present the media has tended to label a wide range of violent acts as terrorism such that the delineation of terrorism is tricky both then and now. But this is a problem with which we have to live and we cannot, as Hoffman tells us, expect a general scientific theory of terrorism. 'A general theory is...impossible because the phenomenon has so many different roots and manifestations.' (1998, p.183) Regardless of such imprecision, it is – to return to the point – with the French revolution that we get the term originally, and where we also see that the unjustifiable has always been 'justified'! In the words of Robespierre:

They say that terrorism is the resort of a despotic government. Is our government then despotism? Yes, as the sword that flashes in the hand of the hero of liberty is like that with which the satellites of tyranny are armed...The government of the revolution is the despotism of liberty against tyranny.

Robespierre in Scruton, 1983, p.546

TERROR IN THE 19TH CENTURY

We shall come back to justifications of terrorism – as problematical as that of Robespierre – when we reach the 20th century. Despite its origins in the state (an important fact that is sometimes forgotten or misinterpreted as we go on to consider) terrorism's 'development' (if that is the right word) during the 19th century had much more to do with individuals, with groups and with attempts to unseat political opponents in power. It is with the 19th century that terrorism arrives first as a word, but then in what we might term 'recognizable' form, though it is still not quite the creature we might imagine today.

Terrorism's early days saw scattered activity which might be labeled as such in countries as diverse as Italy, Spain, Russia, Germany, Ireland and the USA. It was particularly influenced by the activities of Italians and Germans. One such example would be the Italian secret societies working towards unification of that country (achieved in 1871). The activities of these Carbinari are recounted by Bartoldi. Laqueur's contemporary account notes that they were pitiless revolutionaries, ready to kill anyone and that membership meant being swallowed up by the whole, losing all ties with family and individual identity (1979). Individual Carbinari were expected to commit whatever was required of them and the group used highly bloodthirsty language. This group, and fear of them, demonstrates the extent to which a mythology can grow up around terrorists; the Carbonari claim a place in legend although their violence was rarely coordinated and organized and its impact not tremendous at more than the individual level. But their very secretness – with origins still unclear, though suspected as being in Naples at the turn of the 19th century (with possible inspiration from anti-Austrian secret societies or the French Revolution) – make them much more significant than the mere perpetrators of random violence. It is clear nonetheless, that we are dealing with a qualitatively different creature from the modern techno-terrorist. It was an Italian also, Camille Pisacane who developed the idea of 'propaganda by deed' (Hoffman, 1998, p.17) which was to be important as an idea in many countries during the 19th century and which encapsulated the 'romantic' idea that a single person, acting with altruistic heroism and violence, could bring about big changes.

Another Italian, Pisacane developed the idea of 'propaganda by deed' (Hoffman, 1998, p.17) which was to be important as an idea in many countries during the 19th century.

Another important 'ideas man' in this evolution was the German socialist Wilhelm Weitling (1808-71) who heavily influenced anarchist writer Mikhail Bakunin and who contributed ideas on 'direct action'. (See Laqueur, 1979). Weitling offered a typically self-serving phrase when justifying terror as 'founding the kingdom of heaven by unleashing the furies of hell.' Another German of the time, Karl Heinzen (1809-80) argued in *Der Mord* (Murder) that 'while murder was forbidden in principle this prohibition did not apply to politics.' (in Laqueur, 1987, p.27–8).

With the partial exception of the activities of the Italian unificationists, the concept of the systematic use of terrorism really comes to the fore in the 1870s and with the writings of Russian revolutionaries. Key writers here were Nechaev and Bakunin and an organization called Narodnaya Volya who put into practice Pisacane's propaganda by deed. But just as the Tsarist system they sought to depose was not nearly so despotic and ruthless as later Stalinism (see Chapter 5), so the Narodnaya Volya seem almost nice by today's apparently ruthless standards. Those behind the Lockerbie bombing of 1988 for instance killed 270 innocent people. Nikolai Morozov and Tarnovski who plotted and killed the Tsar in 1881, aborted a first attempt to do so because the Tsar had unexpectedly appeared with his children. In what is perhaps a lesson for today's war on terrorism, Russian authorities were ultimately able to extinguish Narodnaya Volya's terrorist network but failed to address the reasons for its original existence: the re-emergence of revolutionary violence four decades later led directly to the establishment of the Soviet Union.

At this time terrorism really was somewhat more of a symbolic threat than anything else. It failed to achieve much beyond the distribution of pamphlets and the dissemination of the idea that a few brave men acting alone could make a real difference. Indeed, in subsequent revolutions this actually proved to be the case and at the time even the vague talk, or myth, of global revolutionary pretensions was enough to frighten the powers that be. There is actually evidence that such fear was used and amplified to assist in social control and that 'the great international anarchist conspiracy existed only in the imagination of police chiefs and the press.' (Laqueur, 1987, p.51).

Beyond the cottage industry of pamphlets and influential works such as Kropotkin's *The Spirit of Revolt* and Johann Most's German language paper *Freiheit* (published in London) terrorism was not a big phenomenon, but it was gaining an intellectual, moral and philosophical basis. Johann Most was born in Germany in 1846 and served an apprenticeship as a bookbinder. He was forced to leave Germany after Bismarck's emergency anti-Socialist laws and ended up in London. Most used the phrase 'humanity through barbarism' and suggests that some 'innocents' were bound to get hurt in the process, although he felt this ought not to be an undue distraction.

Looking at 19th century terror, we can see the modern phenomenon in embryonic form and some parallels or dangers for today. Can we defeat terrorism by simply repressing it or do such efforts simply strengthen the monster? To sum up pre-20th century terrorism we can say that the idea took a hold and the word itself gained currency. Various revolutionaries and anarchists of all stripes pondered its efficacy and its use began to spread. With time it certainly changed, but, in essence, its form and tactics came to resemble something similar to that which we see today, though they were on a smaller local or national scale.

THE 20TH CENTURY FACE OF TERRORISM

An example of terrorism becoming more like its contemporary self can be seen in Indian terrorism of the early 20th century. This had some interesting characteristics, including that it now moved away from the predominant anarchism and came in various types, some factional, others nationalistic or socialist. Eschewing the care which had been demonstrated by Narodnaya Volya, Indian attacks often resulted in the deaths of innocent bystanders, as this could now be justified on the grounds that 'reason' had forced them into it. What else could they do? What crime was there that the British had not committed in India? This was seen as lashing out at the evil and unyielding empire where terror was the only route open.

The Indian 'Philosophy of the Bomb' declared that 'terrorism instils fear in the hearts of oppressors, it brings hope of revenge and redemption to the oppressed masses. It gives courage and self-confidence to the wavering, it shatters the spell of the subject race in the eyes of the world, because it is the most convincing proof of a nation's hunger for freedom.' (in Laqueur, 1987, p.47).

So then, as now, terrorism, however unfeeling, was certainly not unthinking; evil perhaps, but not pure evil. Evil diluted with logic, with reason and, from a certain perspective, necessity; the only apparent option? After bombing the legislative assembly in Delhi in 1929, Bhagat Singh and Batukeswar Datta made no attempt to escape saying, quite calmly and logically, that it had simply been their (only) means of giving expression to the agony of those who had no voice.

So, for all the historical ideas on which we can draw in analyzing terrorism, it is, in many senses, a 20th century phenomenon. In a way this can be traced to the rise of democracy. Whilst absolute rulers ruled absolutely and often brutally, the consequences of rebellion were great and the possibility of organizing it remote. Terrorism was isolated and easily repressed with brutality. With the rise of democracy in the 19th century and then the spread of universal suffrage during the 20th century, people have become used to the idea of having a say. In the past 'minorities had been oppressed, nations had been denied independence, autocratic government had been the rule. But as the ideas of enlightenment spread and as the appeal of nationalism became increasingly powerful, conditions that had been accepted for centuries became intolerable.' (Laqueur, 1987, p.15).

Concurrently, urbanization meant people were less tied to the land. Previous notions that life was a recurring cycle were thus replaced by the idea that life was about progress and that people had a right to a say in how this progress would come about and what shape it would take. With these freedoms came the freedom to use violence as a form of social protest where progress was stifled by those in power, where progress was thought to be moving in the wrong direction or, in some cases, where progress was not seen as a positive thing at all. In other words, people who felt they had no other means of changing a situation were more easily able to resort to violence as a means of redress.

But initially at least, protest mainly took the form of complaint about who was in charge of where. In other words, 'from the turn of the century to the 1960s, terrorism was mainly the preserve of nationalist-separatist movements.' (Laqueur, 1979, p.117). Although one could qualify this in several ways – and certainly the activities of Hitler and Stalin occupy us in the subsequent chapters – what this basically means is that terrorism was normally carried out by people seeking their own country. Here we are talking about the situation in Ireland, in Macedonia, and in Palestine for instance. In such cases, the treatment of those seeking their own country was undoubtedly an important factor in stimulating violence, but the basis of it was the desire for a homeland to be ruled by and for themselves. When looking back into what might almost be called the pre-history of several contemporary 'situations' we can easily see how what may now seem – for individual protagonists or interested outsiders – as a clear cut case of them and us, or of good against evil, from historical perspective becomes very much more difficult to understand in such straightforward terms.

Though we shall refer to various Palestinian groups in chapter 3, and the response with which they are currently met in chapter 5 on state terror, it is worth going back a little to see where the events which cause distress as we see them today have their roots. These roots stretch back and have such depth that understanding rather than condemnation will surely be the first step anyone takes to overcoming terrorism. After looking at Palestine we look here at Ireland and, briefly, Macedonia. These are chosen as illustrative examples but in the overall history of terrorism, it is worthwhile bearing in mind that each 'terrorist situation' also has its own history and 'logic'. A brief look at a couple of particularly polarized situations helps to reveal how crucial it is to have a full understanding of the situation. As US funders of the IRA have found, in the aftermath of 11 September, you are either genuinely against the death of innocents or you are not.

THE PALESTINIAN SITUATION

'The Today Programme' on BBC Radio 4 in the United Kingdom, and serious news programs around the world, give quite a lot of coverage to ongoing events in Palestine. What did or did not happen in Jenin? Why do people strap explosives to themselves and then detonate them, killing themselves and as many innocents as possible? The answers to these questions are usually starkly polarized; those providing the answers, from either 'side', never seem to recognize that the other side, too, may have their point of view; this failure stems from the belief that this 'other point of view' is so completely wrong and evil (as against good and right) that it is not worth considering. We would argue that any kind of look into the history of the current situation makes it abundantly clear that it is by no means so simple as it is often represented.

In fact, despite the simple pronouncements of good and evil, it would take a whole book to even begin to get at the vaguest idea of the complexity of the Arab-Israeli situation, which belies the simplicity with which belligerents so easily castigate their opponents. (see Ovendale, 1992). Although in a sense it is surprisingly simple. The historical state of Palestine occupies land where many Jews feel religion justifies the existence of their own state. When the latter replaced the former, reducing Palestinian 'territory' to 22%, resentment of those with historical claims was high against those with religious ones. Since then Israelis have sought their own security through illegal settlements in that 22%, filling it also with roadblocks and turning 'Palestine' into a series of isolated ghettoes with little hope of improvement. Alas, heavy-handed attempts at security of this kind provoke a backlash.

In order to get to the above state of affairs, however, external factors have played a significant role too. Palestine was a UN-mandated territory of Britain. The British Empire had a large Muslim population and promised the Palestinians that they would not be abandoned. In terms of US internal politics, with the emerging power having high concentrations of Jewish citizens in certain parts of its Eastern coast but also with sections of anti-Semitic feeling, there were complicated and confused reactions to Palestine/Israel. Events in Germany, Poland, and the Ukraine in the 1930s and 1940s were also of considerable significance in engendering a collective sense of guilt in Europe and thus sympathy for the idea of a Jewish state.

Jewish immigration into Palestine from Germany rose from 353 people in 1932 to 5392 in 1933, the year that Adolf Hitler became Chancellor and persecution of the Jewish population began to dramatically increase. Overall Jewish immigration into Palestine also rose, quite significantly, and from less than ten thousand in 1932, it was more than thirty thousand in 1933 and 61844 by 1935. Such immigration led to a certain antagonism with local Arabs, especially as the local Jewish Agency had a policy of employing only Jewish labour. Arab riots in September and October of 1933 became an Arab rebellion with secret societies formed, sometimes inspired then, as some are now, by the duty of jihad or holy war.

Britain failed to stop immigration of Jews into its Palestinian mandated territories. For this the Arabs assumed Britain to favour a Zionist policy. (The word Zionist – describing the movement for the establishment of Jewish homeland or state in Palestine – has its origins in the late 19th century when it was used by Nathan Birnbaum although it relies on much older historical, primarily religious arguments). Arab fears were heightened by other factors; the future British war hero Captain Orde Wingate, a proponent of Zionism, is said to have led 'special night squads' of mixed British and Zionist Units against Arab rebels and incidentally (but of course) to protect a pipeline of the Iraq Petroleum Company. Like the death squads which exist today in Colombia and elsewhere, Orde Wingate's methods were ruthless and certainly terrorist. To the Arabs this undoubtedly appeared as an alliance between Britain and the Zionists. (Ovendale, 1992, p.76), leaving the Arab population disgruntled at immigration and collaboration between the Jews and British.

Living in harmony was not really considered an option at any point. Potential partition of the area as two states was ruled out early on as uneconomic and may have proved a fraught business, especially over the still vital issue of water. At the very minimum it would also have caused the widespread movement of population. With this option 'rejected' as a given, the Jewish Agency (or government) resolved that if it could not get land in Palestine through legitimate means it would get it in other ways. If arms were forbidden it would train the Haganah, or Jewish army, illegally and if immigration were reduced officially it would bring people in illegally. The strong Zionist movement was determined to succeed.

Despite the Arab perception of Jewish-British collaboration, this tantamount declaration of war on Britain did not sit well with many in the foreign office. In the late 1930s, they were further influenced by George Antonius' paper 'The Arab Awakening'. In it, he points out the moral outrage of making Arabs in Palestine bear the burden of Hitler's persecution. He argued that 'the persecution of one people could not be justified to relieve that of another'. (Antonius, 1938). It seemed that Europe was allowing the Arabs to bear the weight of their collective guilt. Faced by such an apparent shift in sympathy against Zionism, Ovendale argues that the Zionists began to put into practice their effective declaration of war. On February 27 1939 thirty-eight Arabs died in a series of bomb explosions for instance.

Whereas in the early thirties the Zionists had the ear of the British, from the middle of the decade and beyond British imperial interests (an empire containing many Muslim subjects) began to exert ever more influence on British policy. As the paramount regional power at that time Britain was able to move ahead with a conciliatory policy towards the Arab population. In response then, Zionists – the founders of modern Israel – responded with terror aimed at wearing down British morale. Many recent Israeli politicians were first terrorists. The murder of British policemen and assassination attempts became the norm. On 6 November 1944 Lord Moyne, the Minister resident in the Middle East was murdered in Cairo by the underground Jewish terrorist group, the Stern gang.

Zionist terrorist elements such as the Stern Gang and Irgun gained encouragement from pro-Zionist policy statements emerging in the USA at this time. These statements actually had to do with US domestic politics as much as genuine pro-Zionism; they emerged due to both the influence of a large Jewish lobby and, ironically, the anti-Semitic feeling which saw the USA favouring further immigration into Palestine as an alternative to further Jewish immigration into the USA. The Stern Gang and Irgun, in their training 'essentially totalitarian', and highly committed, would stop at nothing to overthrow the British administration.

However, Zionist resolve also coincided with Arab leader Ibn Saud, founder of the kingdom of Saudi Arabia, telling President Roosevelt how Arabs would rather die than yield land to the Jews. It was an explosive mix. Irgun, led by Menachem Begin, and the Stern Gang threatened to join forces with the Jewish army (Haganah) if Britain attempted to curtail immigration. Haganah realized the value of such terrorist allies. The Jewish Agency was also implicated in an increasingly united Zionist position. While the Americans saw the situation in terms of New York elections the British resolve was weakened by the death of British soldiers. Although Zionist propaganda suggested that settlement in Palestine was considered the only option by many Jewish refugees in Europe, the Arabs – not unreasonably – asked if there was 'any reason why they, the one race with no anti-Semitic tradition, should have to bear the sins of Christian Europe.' (Ovendale, 1992, p.104). It was surely not an unreasonable point. At a later conference an Iraqi asked if Arab peoples were to be the only ones asked to pay for what Hitler had done to the Jews.

Whilst the domestic concerns of the USA and Britain clashed on the ground (Truman appeared to support Zionism while its terrorists murdered British soldiers), so did the complex historical, moral, religious, legal, economic and social claims of both Jews and Arabs. It was certainly complicated but there is no doubt that those working for the establishment of Israel had amongst their number a significant contingent of what may only be described as terrorists. Kidnappings were common.

Jerusalem's King David Hotel – part of which acted as British Army HQ – was blown up by Irgun/Haganah killing ninety-one.

With time, and with further Jewish immigration, the tide seemed slowly to move with the Zionists. Privately, President Truman wrote that the Zionists 'seem to have the same attitude towards the "underdog" when they are on top as they have been treated as "underdogs" themselves.' He continued, 'I suppose that is human frailty'; as is supposing that your own terror is justified whilst condemning that of others, apparently (see Ovendale, p.109). A state founded on terrorism now fails to understand the motivation of others, and justifies its own well-documented oppression as counter-terrorism.

In late 1946 a Zionist terrorist too young to hang was given eighteen years and eighteen strokes of the cane by the British authorities. Begin's Irgun, outraged, responded by kidnapping four British officers and giving each of them 18 lashes of the whip. Britain executed several Zionist terrorists. In retaliation Irgun hanged two British sergeants and booby-trapped their bodies. An eye for an eye. Very often two eyes for an eye. A thousand eyes for an eye. As also in Northern Ireland, to which we move next, the situation is complicated because Zionist terrorists received much funding from the USA. Twenty British soldiers died in a Jerusalem Officer's club and the Prime Minister publicly protested that arms for such acts were being supplied by the US. The profits from Hecht's Zionist musical A Flag is Born went straight to Irgun as a tax-free charitable donation. In Britain, public opinion blamed the Americans. Indeed everybody blamed everybody else. Zionist propaganda turned the King David Hotel bombing into an instance of British anti-Semitism rather than a terrorist atrocity. Only 'we', it seems, are ever justified in the terrorist mind.

As British resolve weakened and the reality of US power began to dawn, a Jewish state looked ever more likely, despite Arab protests in the region. Bevin, the British Foreign Secretary wondered aloud whether 'American policy was to allow no Arab country to help their fellow Arabs anywhere, while the United States assisted the Zionists to crush the Arabs within Palestine and to allow the slaughter to continue;' but Britain was not powerful enough for more than such verbal protests. 127 dead and 331 soldiers wounded in less than two years prevented, in any case, much of a stomach for a fight of any kind. 1800 years of Palestine's history provided no more powerful an argument either. The first Arab–Israeli war began.

On 9 April contingents of the Irgun and the Stern gang, under Haganah command, encountered strong Arab resistance in the village of Deir Yassin, and slaughtered 245 men, women and children, most of the inhabitants of the town.

The Arabs retaliated on 13 April and besieged a convoy of mainly Jewish doctors and nurses on the road to Mount Scopus: seventy seven were killed. (Ovendale, 1992, p.135)

Plus ça change. The Jewish state of Israel was brought about. It does not justify the ongoing terror tactics today by Israelis or Palestinians, but merely amplifies the context to say that in 1946 there were 226,000 Jewish refugees in Europe. By 1949 the number of Palestinian Arab refugees was almost 1 million. The American press hardly mentioned this at all. Is it possible to right wrongs by doing wrong? Surely not, which ever way round we look at the problem.

The foregoing is not the authoritative account of everything that happened in terms of Palestine and the formation of Israel. But this pre-history of what happens today surely asks some significant questions. Perhaps most significantly, why is it acceptable to use terrorism to found an Israeli state but unacceptable to fight the profound injustices of that state? If the only answer is religion how can we combat the theocratic fascism of Al-Qaeda? Why don't the actions of the Israeli Army in any way constitute terrorism despite the massive oppression and suffering they have caused? Can terrorism really be so selective, or shouldn't we look instead to a more objective measure, such as the number of innocent people who get caught in its cross-fire? Surely it is irrelevant whether they were deliberately targeted or just happened to be in a building hit by a missile?

NORTHERN IRELAND

In terms of historical complexity, much the same can be said of Northern Ireland as of Palestine. The 'troubles' dating back a little over three decades have a clear and relevant pre-history going back many, many centuries. This pre-history includes cruel and selfish rule on behalf of a few English (absentee) landowners, mass starvation, anti-Catholic laws and practices and so on. To look at this history in a little more detail shows how recent terrorism in Northern Ireland, from either side of the Catholic/Protestant divide is, though not excusable, certainly explicable and in some senses perfectly understandable, perhaps, alas, inevitable.

This complex history can, indeed, be taken back a long way. The Irish are different from the English, as Kevin Kelley points out, and not being a part of the Roman Empire can be cited as just one example of why this might be so. From the time of the Normans, England fought battles for control with the local Gaelic population, ultimately leaving England only a toehold around Dublin which was itself besieged by rebellions throughout the 15th and 16th centuries. A particularly serious uprising of 1534 during the reign of Henry VIII was suppressed with the kind of brutality which has often characterized and coloured Anglo-Irish relations and perceptions.

Historical differences and animosities were extended as England became part of the Protestant reformation whilst the Gaels remained resolutely Catholic. At the same time, English attempts to control Ireland, gradually and brutally gained ground and, ironically enough in terms of the current situation, only the northern province of Ulster remained an un-subdued Gaelic stronghold at the end of the 16th century. This resistance, and the reactions to it, are both crucial in terms of the current 'troubles'.

After Britain finally gained control of all Ireland around 1600 – with the leading rebellious O'Neill and O'Donnell clans going into exile – it resolved to poison the roots of rebellion, encouraging the systematic 'planting' of English and Scottish (Protestant) settlers. And initially it worked; Antrim and Down were secured. However, by 1641 another rebellion was underway, this time aimed directly at the new settlers themselves. Henceforth, of course, they would see themselves as a besieged minority who must look to England for protection against the Catholic hordes!

Then, after the interruption of civil war was over in England, Cromwell embarked upon an exceptionally cruel re-conquest or 'reordering' in Ireland. Many Irish were sold into slavery and Catholicism was crushed mercilessly. By the time James II took to the throne of England, Catholics owned little land (confiscated to pay the New Model Army) and were predominantly agricultural laborers. Later an apartheid-like system – the Penal Laws – was introduced, with Anglicans guaranteed special privileges while Catholics were consigned to inferiority; an eldest son could now only inherit land if he converted to Protestantism. Catholics were not permitted to teach, to vote, to obtain public employment, to own a firearm nor to openly practice their religion.

By the 18th century, and as Britain sought an Empire abroad, Ireland was clearly seen as the agricultural supplier in the imperial scheme to be exploited with no thought given to the domestic population. By 1750, George Berkeley (Protestant Bishop of Cloyne) asked 'whether there be upon the earth any Christian or civilized people so beggardly wretched and destitute as the common Irish?' (Kelley, 1988, p.7). Bands of peasants began launching desperate terrorist attacks faced with such conditions.

Against such a background, some – Gratton and Tone for instance – dreamed of an Ireland united, not on the basis of religion, but as a nation free to make its own choices and to prosper. Although some of these dreams were 'bourgeois' – based upon the wishes of the wealthy to trade upon better terms – others included alliances of the downtrodden masses regardless of religious difference. Crucially however a Protestant (Anglican) elite and a Britain using classic colonial 'divide and rule' tactics were able to stifle such aspirations. The newly formed Orange Order, still significant today, sought to drive a sectarian wedge between Catholics and Presbyterians, though on opportunistic rather than religious grounds. Previously the Presbyterian dissenters had found common ground in oppression and poverty with Catholics but were encouraged to emphasize difference instead. In this way Irish politics, and more particularly northern Irish politics have been characterized by an absence of class alliances which might otherwise have seen religious differences dissolve. A century after its formation, James Connolly, an Irish socialist, was able to analyze the purpose of the Orange Order as having been to deny religious freedom but to raise religious questions in the service of oppressive – and Anglican favouring – property rights.

In 1798 Tone had sought to go to the source of the problem as he saw it, enlisting the help of the French revolutionaries against England. However his rebellion was let down by the French and about 50,000 Irishmen died in the fighting and subsequent reprisals in a brave but futile gesture. England responded in 1800 by closing the Dublin Parliament, formalizing 'Union' and suggesting that Catholics could now sit at Westminster. This latter point was forgotten and money was provided to Presbyterian congregations to stop any continuing tendency to unite with Catholics. As Kelley observes, 'this money was instrumental in checking the radical impulse of Presbyterianism and in coaxing dissenters to align with Anglicans in order to defend the Union against Catholic attack.' (1988, p.12). Tone was hanged, repression against Catholics was high and Union seemed strong, so it is significant that even in this darkest hour of republicanism men such as Robert Emmet were still prepared to attempt rebellion and martyr themselves in the process.

From this point onwards the history of Ireland seems to be one of (further) English arrogance, (further) Irish suffering and the shameless exploitation of religious difference by those in power. O'Connell's appeals for Catholic emancipation ignored the plight of poor Presbyterians whilst he himself was anti-labour, thus inflaming differences. The idea of 'Protestant supremacy' became a key theme in Belfast along with sectarian street-fighting; the Dickensian lives lived by all brought no class alliance because Protestants simply feared Catholics would seize their meagre wage.

Queen Victoria is reputed to have said 'The Irish people ['her' people] are a really shocking abominable people, not like any other nation.' The potato famine – an English 'invention' by contemporary accounts – led into a latter part of the 19th century where evictions and insecure tenure typified life for many such that terrorist attacks were the only effective option available to those dispossessed.

By the late 1800s the idea of 'home rule' had become widely supported in Ireland, except in Ulster (Northern Ireland) where (relative) prosperity had come to be seen as dependent upon a secure place within the British Empire and where religious differences had been particularly manipulated, with poor Protestants constantly seeing their situation in comparison to that of the Catholic minority. The Tories, as well, for self-interested and chauvinist reasons, opposed home rule. Randolph Churchill, that most rabid of Tory leaders went to Belfast in 1886, encouraging his Protestant listeners 'to resort to extra constitutional methods – i.e. armed resistance – should that prove to be the only way of overcoming Gladstone's connivance with the home rulers.' (Kelley, 1988, p.24).

So, whilst in England, Scotland and Wales workers began to realize that they had a common bourgeois enemy, in Ulster industrial peace was preserved by Protestant determination to preserve an edge over fellow toilers who happened to be Catholic. As Gaelic pride swelled elsewhere in Ireland (Sinn Fein was formed), in Ulster the loyalists resolved to fight attempts to force them into a republic. Without going into the compromise, and one might add continued anti-Catholic prejudice, which led to the troubles in the north, it is clear that whatever the outcome of the current peace process, at their base the 'troubles' emerge not from some random pathological desire to maim and use violence but from centuries of extremely complex patterns of politics and oppression which make the attitudes on either side comprehensible if not reasonable.

MACEDONIA

The cases of both Palestine and Northern Ireland illustrate how terrorism, condemned as pointless, cruel and tragic may indeed be all these things, but that part of the tragedy lies in the inability of one group of people to recognize the logic of another group of people once they feel they have been given no other recourse than to lash out in a violent way. But it would not be accurate simply to say that all terror has a complicated history and that if we look into it we shall find rationale and explanation. Indeed what we can more easily say is that generalization is phenomenally difficult. Terrorism is often – as in Palestine and Northern Ireland a complicated but largely zero-sum game – but it is rarely the same 'game', and not always of that type at all. Another relatively well-known example of terrorism in the late 19th and early 20th centuries concerns the situation in the Balkans.

The area of present day Macedonia (or the Former Yugoslav Republic of Macedonia, to give it its full title), and the surrounding much larger area which was historically called Macedonia, were for many hundreds of years under uniform rule and very much multi-cultural in make up. So the Macedonian dynasty of Vassilius the first and second in the 11th Century, the Byzantine Empire and, in the 17th and 18th centuries, the Ottoman Empire ruled over disparate territories in the area which were not ethnically homogenous and where people were most likely to identify on the basis of religion rather than taking notice of ethnic identity or any sense of 'nationality'. Yes there were, by today's standards, Bulgarian kingdoms to the north of a region known as Macedonia, Slavs in the south and many fragmented Greek peoples, but by and large these peoples were not demanding unitary states on ethnic lines and Macedonia, whilst a distinct geographical term, was something akin to 'East Anglia' or the 'Mid West'; it existed of course, and the people who lived there could have a name attached to them on that basis but it was hardly a name that would inspire people to resort to terror in order to bring about a state.

To this area of fragmented, religious-based affinities came ideas from the Enlightenment period of European history and examples in the form of both US and French revolutionaries. A 19th century Serbian peasant revolt failed but again provided an example. At the same time the Ottoman empire was weakening. Greek, Serb and Bulgarian states existed, though not with today's boundaries, but between them was a central area, still Ottoman, and within this the geographical area the region of Macedonia. In this central area people still tended to be not Greek, Slav or Turks but simply Christians. In this context the church became important in beginning to galvanize identities through the Bulgarian church, Greek church and so on. In the 19th century the area was characterized by the presence of irregular bands and incursions and a very unclear situation.

Out of this mix emerged the IMRO, Internal Macedonian Revolutionary Organization (or VRMO in Greek). The emergence of this organization was complex, the height of its influence brief, and its descent into criminal activity confusing from the point of view of whether to define it still as terrorist. The history of 'Macedonia' is far too complex to have encapsulated here, and controversial enough that this abbreviated account will have offended all sides to the argument, but for the interested reader it provides an example of the complexity of terrorism beyond

the 'them and us' dynamic of Israel and Palestine. Having outlined some complex cases with roots in the early 20th century
and beyond it is time to move nearer to the present.

THE 1960S AND ONWARDS

Terrorism as social protest began to emerge in the 1960s on a relatively small scale amongst left wing groups. Although Walter
Laqueur has argued that 'the publicity accorded to their actions
was in inverse proportion to their real importance' (1979, p.119)
this may be underestimating what was going on. For a start such
groups encouraged other groups; particularly in Latin America
they encouraged a brutally violent right-wing backlash, not just
against the terrorists but against the wider population and
anyone seen as supporting similar aims of social change. Alas,
this (over) reaction – in many cases helped by US funding and
training – stimulated further protest, boosted the numbers associated with terrorism (or guerrilla warfare) and led to a large
number of deaths. In some cases, as we shall see, the process
ended in full-scale civil wars or revolutions because rather than
a 'political' response, demands had met with violence. Of course
the argument can be made that 'dealing politically' with terrorism is akin to 'negotiating' with terrorists and should not be
countenanced. However, the spiral of violence often associated
with terrorism may be a worse error, and is something we
should be particularly preoccupied with today.

But where does the spiral start? In the 1960s the intellectual
community of Peace Research and Conflict Studies (especially
in Scandinavia and North America) was particularly concerned
with this question. The peace researchers argued that peace
could be seen as either 'positive' or 'negative'. Negative or
minimal peace was what we might normally understand by the

term; peace in this sense is the situation when there is no war or large scale inter-state violence taking place. However, others argued that to define peace in this way meant that an awful lot of bad things could be happening but still be called peace. In other words, poverty and starvation could be called 'peace'. This they argued was not right. Reflecting some of the philosophical currents of the time, they suggested that peace could not simply be the absence of something bad (war) but had to be the existence of something positive or good. Of course, therein lies the problem. What is positive peace? Without an exhaustive survey, positive peace would be concerned with the existence of a type of society in which people felt happy. Therein lie further problems. Would such a society be based on welfare, for example? What would be the attitude to religious and cultural freedom? Who would pass laws, and how would they be debated and agreed? And so on. Oddly enough, terrorist groups (and states) have effectively decided that the possible future achievement of positive peace means that using violence now can be justified.

Along with this debate about positive and negative conceptions of peace the concept of 'structural violence' was important. Those who put forward this idea argued that it was unsatisfactory to think of violence in terms of merely confrontation. Violence, they argued, occurred not only when a physical blow of some description – a punch, a shot, a bomb – was delivered, but could be concealed in structures for the oppression of particular groups. Put more simply, if I am not happily living in a state of positive peace this may be because I am the victim of the structures of the society in which I live. If I have to work very long hours, in poor conditions, for not very much money I could thus be considered as a victim of the structural violence of capitalism. The idea was used to suggest that countries of the Third

World were victims of the structures of the international economic system. The idea was also useful, of course, in justifying the apparently contradictory idea that violence could, and should, be used to, bring about peace.

What this meant was that terrorist groups could claim that 'terrorism merely opposes violence with violence in the name of freedom from violence.' (Scruton, 1983, p.546). It is simply a question of how one defines violence. There is, however, a flaw. Anyone, living anywhere at any time, could claim that any regime they did not like for whatever reason was inflicting structural violence on them and that they were therefore entirely reasonable in responding with violence. Although that does not sound acceptable, at the same time, in some cases, people's living conditions might very well be described as the intolerable consequence of violence inherent in the system. Emma Goldman was certainly not the only one to claim that where people used violence it was where 'intolerable pressure had driven them to commit acts of despair.' (in Laqueur, 1979, p.183).

As well as groups fighting against the 'irredeemable social and economic inequalities of the modern capitalist liberal democratic state' in more recent history we have seen that terrorism has become associated 'with a type of covert or surrogate warfare whereby weaker states could confront larger, more powerful rivals without the risk of retribution.' (Hoffman, 1998, p.26-7). This highlights that however much we fear terrorism, we ought also to bear in mind that it stems from weakness; and why Hoffman is wrong to use the word 'without'; the risk of retribution has existed and Libya, Afghanistan, the Sudan, and others have paid a price for their involvement, or their suspected involvement, in terrorism.

In the 1970s it was feared that groups of left-wing dissidents and drop-outs would form loose alliances with each other and with states to form a global network of terror. Then as now debate raged as to whether to smash this network or to attack its root causes. In the end, a radical generation of students was replaced by those born into a 'culture of contentment' (Galbraith, 1992) and the end of the Cold War pulled the rug from under left-wing radicalism in general. In effect, within Western countries, the winning of the Cold War won the argument over which sort of society could provide prosperity to its people. But in a world today in which the lack of global prosperity is common knowledge via global media, and where many seek solace in thoughts of the afterlife, how is the West to win the argument against religious fascism if not through creating a more equal world?

CONCLUSION

Though it is rarely taught in this way, the perspective of history can turn massacres into heroic victories and murderers into martyrs. The perspective of history also numbs our immediate horror at actions, turning them into stories almost too ancient to seem real. Sometimes the judgment of history takes a long time to change our perceptions; few would deny that many of the actions of the French revolutionaries were clearly brutal but perhaps even fewer would denounce them, now, as terrorism. From a historical perspective, the overthrow of the ancien regime seems almost inevitable and reasonable. At other times history is much quicker, as in the case of the French resistance in the Second World War, whose status was quickly changed from that given them by the Vichy government, although their methods were in some senses terrorist.

With these points in mind we must surely concentrate our

analysis of terrorism on what people actually do. We all have
political beliefs but the fact that you believe that there are historical and moral claims for a Palestinian state where Israel now
lies does not justify suicide bombings. However, similarly, the
fact that you believe that religious and moral grounds justify the
security of that same state of Israel similarly does not justify terrorism either – even if dressed in the language of so-called
'counter-terrorism' or security. To begin to resolve the issue of
terrorism we must separate cause from effect. If we believe in a
cause but the effects of our, or others', actions are the deaths of
innocent people then we must ask why we are so selective in the
use of the term terrorism.

In the present era, terrorism is as diffuse a concept as it has
ever been and prefixes frequently get attached. Bio-terrorism,
eco-terrorism and narco-terrorism to name but a few. Violence
in the name of more and more causes. How are we to explain
this? Is it linked to ideas expressed by Kennan and by Goldman
(above) that terror is a last resort in the sense that it is used by
people who could choose not to use it but who feel that it is their
only recourse? In the chapters that follow we will say more
about some of the left-wing groups which emerged in the 1960s
and which survive in some form or other. We will also look at
the state-sponsoring of terrorism, both the internal kind of
Stalin and Hitler and the modern variant. In conclusion we will
be asking about the potential terrorism of the 21st century.

Over time terrorism has moved from debates over tyrannicide (or removing a despotic ruler), to debates over social
conditions and through nationalistic and political demands.
Religion has always been an important element where the
killing of innocents has occurred. A common feature has been
that terrorism (except where used as an explicit state tactic) has

been used by people who through weakness (for whatever reason) have been unable to achieve their aims in another way. It has rarely been used when other avenues have been open. Thus, weakness, not strength, is what motivates the methods of today's terrorists. But while those with wealth and privilege remain apparently indifferent to the plight of the majority, terror can only gain more recruits. If it is so obvious that Western ideals are superior, they should prove it. Many of Skywalker's fellow fighters were killed, but he did not give up fighting the empire.

3 TERRORIST GROUPS

THESE DAYS you would have to be living in a cave not to have heard of the loose terror network of al-Qaeda and almost everybody in the world, it seems, could name Osama bin Laden from his picture. However, as the previous chapter demonstrates, terrorism is a phenomenon with a long and varied history and most people could name several more terrorist groups. Readers from different parts of the globe might also know of the Irish Republican Army (IRA), possibly the Greek group 'November 17', the Basque separatist organization ETA, Peru's Shining Path (Sendero Luminoso) and the Sri Lankan Tamil Tigers. For those whose most important cultural influences centre on the 1970s, then groups such as Baader-Meinhof and the Italian Red Brigade might also be mentioned. The following chapter looks at some of the more notorious groups and individuals that have been labeled terrorist in recent times, as well as examining some of the most important acts perpetrated by those involved in terrorism. If one thing it proves that terrorism is a global phenomenon. If some leaders and news coverage suggest that terrorism is concentrated largely in one corner of the world and with one cause – anti-Western – that is clearly not the case when looking at the number of groups and the different causes they espouse. In fact, there are a hell (which might be an apposite choice of word) of a lot more organizations out there who are accused of terrorism. The section is divided geographically taking in groups right across the world but starting, for no particular reason, in the Middle East. Before we look at groups, however, we shall begin this section with a look at Carlos the Jackal.

CARLOS THE JACKAL

Although not, strictly speaking, a group, before Osama bin Laden took over the mantle, 'Carlos the Jackal' was probably the most infamous individual terrorist on the planet. Throughout his career Carlos – whose real name was Illich Ramirez Sanchez – was said to be the terrorist mastermind behind a number of bombings, hijackings and kidnappings across Europe all in his pro-Palestinian cause. He is thought to be the 'godfather' behind the murders of Israeli athletes at the Munich Olympics in 1972 and was involved in the 'Black September' attacks. He seized 70 hostages at a meeting of oil ministers at the Organization of Petroleum Exporting Countries (OPEC) in Vienna in 1975. Three people were killed during the attack, some personally by Carlos, and he escaped after negotiating a deal with the Austrian authorities. He took hostages, including 11 OPEC ministers, to Algeria. The ministers were eventually released unharmed but the event helped seal Carlos's reputation and he was variously described by his prisoners as 'psychotic', 'ruthless', 'cold-blooded' and 'polite'. In the same year he killed two French secret agents and a fellow Lebanese revolutionary in a shooting in Paris. He was also a terrorist for hire. Carlos has reportedly worked for Libya, Syria, Cuba, and groups such as the Popular Front for the Liberation of Palestine (PFLP), the Red Brigade and Baader Meinhoff, though not all of this has been proven.

He was also blamed for shooting and wounding the Jewish president of Marks and Spencer in London and was responsible for a grenade attack on the British headquarters of an Israeli bank. In 1982 he masterminded a car bombing in the centre of Paris which killed one and injured 63. His attacks took place throughout the 1970s and 1980s and despite a worldwide manhunt for Carlos he remained at large for decades. Throughout this time one enduring image of Carlos circulated the world – a picture of him with thick-rimmed glasses staring with no expression towards the camera. His reign of terror came to an end in the 1990s, however, and he is currently serving a sentence of life imprisonment in a French jail. He remained unrepentant when sentenced. He left the courtroom shaking his fist in the air and claimed prison did not worry him. 'They want to sentence me to life in prison. I'm 48 years old so it could be another 40 or 50 years. That doesn't horrify me.' For good measure he added, 'Viva la revolucion.'

Despite his Palestinian sympathies, Carlos was in fact Venezuelan. He was born in Caracas on October 12, 1949. Politics played an early role in his life. His mother, Elba, was a strict Catholic and wanted to give him a name in accordance with her religious beliefs. His father, Jose, though was a devout Marxist and as Carlos was his first son demanded that his name had a revolutionary connotation. So it was that he was called Illich after Vladimir Illich Ulyanov: Lenin. (This set the tone for a new family tradition. His first brother, born two years after Carlos was named Lenin. His second brother born in 1958 was called Vladimir. Carlos later criticized his father for using the names. 'It was bloody stupid of my father to give his children such weird names. That kind of thing weighs on children. In my case it was fortunate, but things were different for my brothers. They are not ashamed of their names, but it did cause them problems in later life,' he said.

His childhood and youth seemed to be marked by the private battling of his mother and father to get their baby boy to follow their preferred path, Christianity or Marxism. Carlos though at first followed his mother's influential path rather than his father's. She had him baptized in secret and took him to mass unbeknown to Jose. His wealthy lawyer father at the same time was teaching him the doctrines of Marxism and told his son tales of South American revolutionaries. He even hired private tutors to complete his son's political education. In his youth his father had been expelled from his home state for harboring a communist outlaw. Angered by the authority's decision he fled to Colombia where he became a committed Marxist. Showing how important politics and religion were in the make-up of life in Carlos's family, his father had entered a Catholic seminary intent on becoming a priest before finally renouncing religion in favour of politics.

Carlos's grandfather Luis was strict on his sons and even wrote a pamphlet of ethical behavior for them to follow. Unfortunately Jose did not follow it himself and after his constant womanizing became unbearable, Elba left the house taking her three sons with her first to Jamaica then Mexico before returning home. By the age of 14 Illich was a member of the Venezuelan Communist Party. After his parents split, Carlos was sent abroad to finish his schooling, ending up rather improbably in Kensington in the mid-1960s. His lifestyle in London was less devoted to revolution and rather more to having a good time (though the two need not be mutually exclusive). After London he was a graduate of the Patrice Lamumba University, in Moscow. And after the USSR, he reportedly moved to Jordan where his initial training as a terrorist took place with the PFLP.

Several stories surround the legend of Carlos the Jackal not all of which should be taken at face value. However one theory has it that he took his revenge on the world because of being teased at school. As he got older he put on weight and was nicknamed 'El Gordo' (Fatso). One tale goes he became so exasperated by the constant teasing he screamed at his friends that one day the rest of the world would know his name. Well, he was half-right. The world did get to know about him but not as Illich Ramirez Sanchez but, instead, as Carlos the Jackal.

THE MIDDLE EAST

AL-QAEDA

It seems natural to start any examination of modern day terrorism with a look at al-Qaeda and Osama bin Laden since this group and individual now seem to be blamed by governments for almost every terrorist attack committed. If it has not been perpetrated directly by the al-Qaeda or even by bin Laden, the claim is usually that any attack has, in part, been funded by it or him or even simply inspired by them. Or, failing that, the group that claims responsibility has also received training from al-Qaeda. This may all be true, but whatever the case it has certainly helped propel bin Laden and his group into the status of the planet's Public Enemy Number One.

Unfortunately, for many he has also become a hero, however incomprehensible that might seem. Any discussion of what this group and individual stands for is therefore difficult as there are few people who can have a dispassionate or disinterested view. Here we look therefore at what al-Qaeda and its leader stand for and what their history is.

Its name means 'the Base'. There seems little doubt that the group was established in the late 1980s as part of the Mujahadin struggle to throw the invading Soviet forces out of Afghanistan. The beginnings of the al-Qaeda movement were an attempt to bring together disparate Arab forces that were fighting against the Red Army. Who brought them together though is open to question. The convention has it that it was bin Laden, but recent reports published in the USA show that the Mujahadin were largely an invention of the West, specifically Washington, in order to try and undermine Moscow and give it its own 'Vietnam'. Viewed on that basis the tactic was successful. Just a decade later the USSR was consigned to history and its symbolic withdrawal from an undefeated Afghanistan an enduring sign of the limits of the power of a dying and bankrupt regime. However, history is not one-dimensional, or at least it should not be, and the creation of the Mujahadin has not only hurt the Soviets but also the USA. The West armed, financed and trained the very people that just two decades later would commit the single most infamous act of terror ever and against those who helped give birth to their struggle.

The group has metamorphosed into one that now wants to create a pan-Islamic state and works to overthrow or undermine Western and other 'non-Islamic' interests. It has constantly re-affirmed its belief that the USA should pull its troops out of Saudi Arabia, withdraw its support for Israel and that the USA, and its supporters, should be punished for their crimes against Iraq (although from that should not be deduced, particularly at current times, that Iraq and al-Qaeda are allies or in any way connected; Al-Qaeda is a group largely made of Sunni Muslims, a group that has suffered under the rule of Saddam Hussein).

In 1998, bin Laden published a manifesto that reflected his

philosophies. Among other statements it claimed that: 'We believe that the biggest thieves in the world are Americans and the biggest terrorists on earth are the Americans. The only way for us to defend against these assaults is by using similar means. We do not differentiate between those dressed in military uniforms and civilians. They're all targets in this fatwah,' he said. And also: 'To kill Americans and their allies, both civil and military, is an individual duty of every Muslim who is able, in any country until their armies, shattered and broken-winged, depart all the lands of Islam.'

Currently al-Qaeda is thought to have several thousand members, although any such number is highly speculative. Though it appears to be a highly organized and particularly effective group, it operates on a 'cell' structure meaning that there are many small groups operating in its name and many of those carrying out the work of 'head office' have no idea about who and how many others also work for al-Qaeda. Until recent years it was thought to operate largely out of just a handful of places such as Afghanistan, Sudan or Yemen. This however has not stopped it stretching its network throughout Europe and beyond as the 11 September attack seems to have proved. Now, and maybe because the organization has been scattered in the light of the American-led bombing of the Taliban regime, it appears to be operational right across the globe. Certainly, experts point to the fact that it is well immersed within South East Asia, and the Bali bomb was thought to be linked to al-Qaeda. This provides an example of the fact that although responsibility for the attack was claimed by some other group – Jemaah Islamiah – it is thought by many to have had the hand of al-Qaeda in it.

The organization is also believed to have a presence now in

South America as well as continuing to maintain its established positions across Europe. It is funded through the murky connections of the Bin Laden Group, a construction empire that is said to be worth billions of pounds and from which Osama bin Laden has poured his own money into the organization. This funding has come under increased scrutiny since 11 September 2001 with money laundering and international financial transactions coming under increased scrutiny. It seems however that al-Qaeda has enough resources to continue its operations.

Al-Qaeda is thought to have been responsible for a host of terrorist attacks, both 'successful' and failed. These include the attacks on 11 September, the bombing of the warship the USS *Cole* in 2000 and the bombing of the US embassies in Kenya and Tanzania in 1998 (all of these attacks are discussed below, Chapter Four). It has also been linked to a plan to assassinate the Pope whilst he was touring the Philippines in 1994. A similar plan was hatched to kill President Bill Clinton a year later as well as a plan to bomb Los Angeles Airport. In December 2001, an attempt by 'Shoe Bomber' Richard Reid to blow up a passenger airliner bound for the United States was foiled though the link here may simply be one of inspiration.

OSAMA BIN LADEN

Seeing as very few people in the world know the whereabouts of bin Laden, or even if he is alive, we still seem to know a huge amount about him. (Some of the things we 'know' about him can also be dismissed. Some have claimed that he hates all things American including – bizarrely – the Rotary Club and this is why he carries out his attacks).

He is in his mid-40s (he was probably born in 1955), tall – 6ft 5in – incredibly wealthy with a private income estimated at anywhere between £20million and £200 million through his family. He clearly does not hate all things Western; now a global game but first played in England, bin Laden is said to like football (soccer) and to have watched Arsenal FC during his time in London. Many of his messages about imminent attacks have sporting connotations of 'The game is just about to begin' kind of thing. He may, or may not, have been injured in the American bombing of Afghanistan, and therefore may, or may not be receiving treatment for injuries sustained then. Bin Laden may also be a diabetic. He could also be living in Pakistan. He definitely has a curiously gentle voice for one so murderous.

As a child he travelled through the West with his family and has been pictured as a small boy in Sweden. His radicalization seems to have occurred in his teens in Jeddah, Saudi Arabia, the town of his birth and where he seems to have become increasingly interested in the teachings of radical Muslim groups. What we do know is that after the Afghan struggle against the Soviet Union was won he moved to Sudan in 1991 and established three terrorist camps. However he was exiled, because of international pressure on Sudan in 1996 by which time he had also been stripped of his Saudi citizenship. Much of the rest of his time was, apparently, spent in Afghanistan.

ABU NIDAL ORGANIZATION (ANO)

Prior to the emergence of al-Qaeda and Osama bin Laden perhaps the most famous of Islamic terrorist groups was the Abu Nidal Organization (ANO). By some estimates this group has carried out attacks in 20 different countries and killed or injured almost 900 people. These attacks have been carried out on various groups, people and interests including those of the West, fellow Palestinians and in Arab countries. It is linked to the Palestinian struggle for a homeland and split from the Palestinian Liberation Organization (PLO) in 1974. It has also been known by various different names including the Fatah Revolutionary Council, the Arab Revolutionary Brigades and probably most famously Black September (see below).

It is thought to be led by Sabri al-Banna and is located across parts of the Middle East. It has camps in Lebanon's Bekaa Valley and supporters among Palestinian refugee camps in the same country. Sudan and Syria are thought to provide havens for ANO operatives and previously it also operated out of Libya. Training and financial assistance was given by Libya and Syria as well. However as the Tripoli regime has moved slowly back into the international fold following the tortuous discussions over Lockerbie, the ANO's ability to operate in that country was severely limited and has now been halted. Membership of the ANO numbers somewhere around the 200 mark.

The ANO was responsible for attacks on Rome and Vienna airports in December 1985, the Pan Am flight 73 hijacking in Karachi in September 1986, and the bombing of a day trip boat in Greece in July 1988. However, this attack was one of the last carried out on Western targets which it has not targeted since the 1980s. The organization, which has a military and political wing was also suspected of assassinating the PLO deputy chief Abu Iyad and its security chief Abu Hul in Tunis in January 1991.

HAMAS (ISLAMIC RESISTANCE MOVEMENT)

The Hamas group has gained international notoriety in its longstanding armed struggle to create an Islamic Palestinian state in the Middle East. It continues to operate, and in November 2002 claimed responsibility for a suicide attack on an Israeli bus in residential Jerusalem, which killed at least 11 people with many of the victims being schoolchildren. It was founded in 1987 and its strength is concentrated in the West Bank and Gaza Strip. But it is not confined to these contentious areas. Support and membership is drawn from Israeli Arabs, neighboring Arab countries – it was only in 1999 that Jordanian authorities closed down the group's office in Amman – including Saudi Arabia, Syria and Iran. It has also raised funds from Europe and the United States (not the governments). As well as being an organization committed to armed struggle it has also committed itself to political action by putting forward candidates in Chamber of Commerce elections held in the West Bank. It also has a strong religious base, as might be guessed from its name, and recruits members through mosques and also tries to raise funds via this method. Although its membership numbers are a matter of conjecture it can be stated quite accurately that it has thousands of supporters in the West Bank and Gaza Strip areas which see its activities as an important bulwark against the work of the Israeli state.

It has carried out a number of high-profile suicide bombings since the 1980s against Israeli interests. The last attack in November 2002 was just the latest in a long-running campaign that has seen many similar attacks launched. As well as targeting Israeli interests both military and civilian it has also murdered suspected Palestinian collaborators and members of the al-Fatah group because of its stance of trying to negotiate a political solution with Israel (see below).

AL-FATAH (AL-ASIFA)

This is the group through which the Palestinian Liberation Organization's (PLO) chief Yasser Arafat first rose to international prominence. In 1968, Arafat led al-Fatah into the PLO. It has been effective in several armed campaigns since that time.

Many of its military leaders resided in Jordan and were instrumental in the Black September attacks of 1970 ('Black September' is used, somewhat confusingly, as a name for a group *and* for a specific set of incidents). Jordanian attacks on Palestinians, many of whom had fled to the country since the establishment of Israel, led to the violent expulsion of many members of al-Fatah as well as events such as the hijacking of Jordanian passenger planes in the same year. After fleeing Jordan, group members fled to other parts of the Middle East including Lebanon. They were on the move again after the Israeli invasion in 1982. Now members of the group are found in Tunisia and Algeria as well as re-locating back in Lebanon after the country's fragile return to peace. Its current headquarters are in Tunis. Its history is a constant round of shifting alliances. It has previously received support from Saudi Arabia, though this changed after the Gulf war of 1991, and from the former Eastern European bloc states, as well as weaponry provided from China and North Korea. Its strength numbers some 7,000, and it is thought to have offered and supplied training to a wide range of other terrorist groups throughout the 1970s. As well as a military arm it has also maintained a political wing whose members have been at the forefront of trying to fashion a political solution to the Palestinian struggle. In 1993, Yasser Arafat signed the Declaration of Principles with Israel, which renounced terrorism. No attacks have been attributed to the group since then.

POPULAR FRONT FOR THE LIBERATION OF PALESTINE

This group is violently opposed to the PLO. Led by Ahmad Jabril, a former captain in the Syrian Army, it has rejected the attempts at a political solution with Israel. It retains close ties with Syria, and retains its headquarters in Damascus though it also has a presence in Lebanon. It was most active in Europe and the Middle East during the late 1970 and early 1980s. It was marked by its highly unusual attacks which included using hot air balloons and motorized hang gliders as a means for launching attacks. Currently it concentrates on small scale attacks in Lebanon and the West Bank and the Gaza Strip. Also thought to be responsible for the 1985 attack on the passenger cruise liner *Achille Lauro* in which one US citizen was murdered.

HEZBOLLAH

One of the most infamous terrorist groups in the Middle East has been active for the past two decades. Its name means the 'Party of God' but it has gone under the title of Islamic Jihad, the Revolutionary Justice Organization and the Organization of the Oppressed on Earth. It was formed in response to the Israeli invasion of Lebanon in 1982. It is based in Lebanon and has taken its inspiration from the former Iranian leader, the Ayatollah Khomeini. Its basic philosophical tenets include the establishment of Islamic rule in Lebanon as well as liberating all occupied Arab lands, including Jerusalem. It has also advanced the idea of the elimination of Israel. It is thought to have received backing from Iran. It is a highly organized group. It has a consultative council (Majlis al-Shura) which is headed up by its leader Hassan Nasrallah. Had expressed its unwillingness to work within the confines of Lebanon's established political system; however, this stance changed with the party's decision in 1992 to participate in parliamentary elections. Subsequently its members won seats to the Lebanese parliament. Although closely allied with, and often directed by, Iran, the group may have conducted operations that were not approved by Tehran. It has several thousand supporters and is thought to have over a hundred terrorist operatives. It continues to receive financial and other support from Iran. Syria is also thought to be a sponsor.

Among the attacks it has claimed responsibility for include the three suicide truck bombings of 1983 in Lebanon although the legitimacy of these claims has been questioned. The attacks were carried out in the name of Islamic Jihad (holy war). The 1983 attacks were followed up with another suicide attack in 1984, for which the same group claimed responsibility. Hezbollah was also thought responsible for the kidnap and murder of Western hostages in the 1980s. Among those it is thought to have taken hostage include Terry Waite. Three members of Hezbollah, Imad Mughniyah, Hasan Izz-al-Din, and Ali Atwa, are on the FBI's list of 22 Most Wanted Terrorists for the hijacking in 1985 of TWA Flight 847 during which a US Navy diver was murdered. In 1992, it moved outside its normal area of activity and attacked the Israeli Embassy in Argentina. Two years later an Israeli cultural centre in the same country was attacked.

KACH AND KAHANE CHAI

Not all terrorist groups within the Middle East are confined to the Palestinian cause. Quite aside from whether or not Israel is a terrorist *state*, a radical terrorist group has emerged sympathetic to the Jewish cause. Kach ('Thus' in Hebrew) and its offshoot Kahane Chai have the stated aims of restoring the biblical state of Israel and expelling Palestinians from that state. Both organizations were founded by US Israeli citizens and indeed members of the same family. Kach was established by Rabbi Meir Kahane. On his assassination in New York in 1990 his son Binyamin founded Kahane Chai – which means Kahane Lives. Binyamin was also to be gunned down. In 2000 he and his wife were killed by Palestinian gunmen in the West Bank. Supporters of his cause have vowed to exact revenge and continue to pursue the policy of the restoration of biblical Israel. Kahane Chai has organized protests against the Israeli government and has threatened Palestinians in Hebron and the West Bank. It is thought to receive funding and support from outside Israel specifically from the United States. In 1994, a Kach supporter, Baruch Goldstein killed 29 Muslim worshippers outside a West Bank mosque, and was himself killed during the attack. The mosque attacked was a particularly sensitive site. It was built above the Cave of the Patriarchs where, according to both Muslim and Jewish traditions, the prophet Abraham is buried. The attacks have not been limited to this one. There have also been further shootings, stabbings and grenade attacks on Palestinians in Jerusalem and the West Bank. Kahane Chai membership is only thought to run into the dozens. Many of its members are thought to be radicalized foreign Jews who have moved to Israel.

ASIA

The terrorist struggle in Asia has in large part centered on India. Not necessarily Indian terror groups, but struggles to do with Indian rule. As well as the assassinations of Indira Gandhi and others there have been other notable events, including the activities of Sikh militants, Kashmir separatists and Tamil separatists opposing the Indian-backed majority rule in Sri Lanka. These are outlined below.

LIBERATION TIGERS OF TAMIL EELAM

Better known as the Tamil Tigers, this group has been involved in a two-decade long struggle to secure an ethnic homeland for

Tamils in Sri Lanka. The group has several other front organizations including the World Tamil Movement, the Ellalan Force and the Sangillan Force. It was founded in 1976 but it was not until 1983 that it took up its armed struggle. It is calculated that 60,000 lives have been lost as well as thousands more people displaced by the struggle. Its attacks include suicide bombings, with the Tamils probably the first to develop jacket bombs worn by individual suicide bombers. Such tactics have been copied by Hezbollah and Hamas. The Tamils claim to represent those people living in the northern and eastern areas of Sri Lanka, mostly in the state of Tamil Nadu, around four million people. Their religion is Hindu, whereas most Sri Lankans, in the Sinhalese population, are Buddhist. Since the 1980s the LTTE (Eelam means homeland in Tamil) have conducted over 200 suicide bombings. These suicide bombers are known as the Black Tigers. This makes it the group that has relied on this tactic more than any other in the world. Among the targets include civilians, office buildings, Buddhist shrines, and a World Trade Center in Colombo, Sri Lanka's capital. The group has also used conventional bombing as well as assassination of leading Sri Lankan officials and civilians. LTTE fighters have also been known to carry cyanide capsules in case they are caught. At full strength it was thought to have around 10,000 armed combatants. Funding is thought to have come through the large displaced Tamil population throughout Europe and North America.

Due to the vast number of suicide attacks carried out the Tamils have gained worldwide notoriety. In May 1991 the LTTE murdered the Indian Prime Minister Rajiv Gandhi at an election campaign rally in India. In May 1993 it assassinated the Sri Lankan President Ranasinghe Premadasa. In July 1999 it assassinated a Sri Lankan MP, Neelan Thiruchelvam, an ethnic Tamil involved in trying to broker a peace deal. Just a few months later it wounded the president Chandrika Kumaratunga and a year later it assassinated the Sri Lankan industry minister C. V. Goonaratne. In December 2001, the Tamils agreed a ceasefire that has been largely kept intact.

HARAKAT UL-MUJAHADIN

This is an Islamic militant group based in Pakistan that operates primarily in Kashmir. It was believed to have close links with al-Qaeda and supported the position of Osama bin Laden in calling for attacks on Western interests. The group operated terrorist training camps in Afghanistan but these were thought destroyed in the US air attacks on Afghanistan in 2001/02.

Its attacks include a number on Indian troops and civilian targets in the disputed region of Kashmir. In July 1995 it was linked to the kidnapping of five Western tourists, all of whom were killed. In December 1999 it pulled off its most notable attack when it hijacked an Indian airliner and forced the release of Masood Azhar (who was in jail in India and a leading figure in the Kashmiri struggle) in return for the release of the 155 hostages taken. At the same time it got the release of Ahmad Omar Sheikh, who, in February 2001 was arrested for the abduction and murder of US journalist Daniel Pearl. The group collected donations from Saudi Arabia and Pakistan, countries thought to be among its major supporters. Many of those involved with this group are veterans of the Afghan struggle against the Soviet Union. At its peak it was thought to have several thousand armed supporters. Following the crackdown on terrorist groups since 11 September by the Pakistani authorities, as Karachi sought to stay on the right side of Washington, its funding and ability to operate is thought to have been radically curtailed. In anticipation of a financial crackdown it had already pulled a lot of its funds out of Pakistani banks.

JAISH-E-MOHAMMED

When Masood Azhar was released from prison he formed Jaish-e-Mohammed (Army of Mohammed), an Islamic extremist group based in Pakistan. The group's aim is to unite Kashmir with Pakistan. The group has subsequently been banned and its assets were frozen by the Pakistani Government in January 2002. In October 2001 the group claimed responsibility for a suicide attack on the Jammu and Kashmir legislative assembly building in Srinagar that killed 31 people. However this claim was later denied by the group's leaders. The Indian Government has also implicated the JEM, for an attack in the same year on the Indian Parliament that killed 9 and injured 18. It is thought to have broad support in the Kashmir area of Pakistan as well as the Southern Kashmir area of India. Once again it is a group that has its origins in the Soviet–Afghan war. Until 2001 it maintained training camps in Afghanistan. It was thought to have very close ties with the Taliban and has received, it is alleged, funding from bin Laden. Like Harakat ul-Mujahadin it anticipated a move to freeze its assets and is believed to have transferred most of its funding outside the banking system before the authorities could get to it.

ABU SAYYAF GROUP

This group has risen to prominence in the last few years in the process of its armed struggle to advance the Islamic cause in the southern Philippines. It claims that its motivation is to promote an independent Islamic state in western Mindanao and the Sulu Archipelago, areas in the southern Philippines heavily populated by Muslims. However, the ASG now appears to use terror mainly for financial profit and can thus be considered an economic/criminal actor as much as a political/terrorist one. It is yet another group thought to be composed of veterans from the Afghan war against the Soviet Union. The group emerged in the early 1990s, a splinter group from the Moro National Liberation Front. Leader of the group is Khadaffy Janjalani. Part of the reason for its rise to prominence in the West in the last few years has been its use of kidnapping as a political tool. Bombings and extortion have also taken place. In April 2000, an ASG faction kidnapped 21 persons, including 10 foreign tourists, from a resort in Malaysia. Separately in 2000, the group abducted several foreign journalists, three Malaysians, and a US citizen. In May 2001, it then kidnapped three US citizens and 17 Filipinos. Several of the hostages were subsequently murdered. It is made up of around 1,000 core fighters and has financed itself through ransom money received. It operates in four regions of the Philippines – Basilan Province, Sulu and Tawi-Tawi and Zamboanga Peninsula. It has also operated outside the Philippines as in Malaysia in 2000.

ISLAMIC MOVEMENT OF UZBEKISTAN

This is a coalition of Islamic groups from Uzbekistan and other Central Asian states that are opposed to the Uzbekistani President Islam Karimov's secular regime. The IMU's primary goal is the establishment of an Islamic state in Uzbekistan and it has sounded an anti-Western and anti-Israeli note in its pronouncements. The Uzbekistani government has, in the past few years, announced that it is worried about the rise of Islamic fundamentalists in the country as well as the action of the 'Wahhabi' sect in Tajikistan and Kyrgyzstan. Its activities have been fairly small scale (compared to some) and in February 1999 it was responsible for five car bombs, which went off in the Uzbekistan capital of Tashkent. The IMU also took foreigners hostage in 1999 and 2000, including four US citizens and four Japanese geologists. Many of its leaders are thought to have been killed or captured since the launch of the 'War on Terror' in October 2001. Its leader Juma Namangani was apparently killed during an air strike in November. It probably has fewer than 2,000 members and garners support from the border areas of Uzbekistan as well as from within the country itself. It has been known to broadcast announcements on Iranian radio hinting that it receives support from there as well.

KURDISTAN WORKERS PARTY/CONGRESS FOR FREEDOM AND DEMOCRACY IN KURDISTAN

To many foreign observers this struggle only became apparent in 1999 after the capture of the group's leader Abdullah Ocalan by the Turkish authorities. This prompted mass demonstrations among ethnic Kurds across Western Europe including infamous scenes of supporters burning themselves in protest at the news. The PKK was founded in 1974 primarily composed of Turkish Kurds. Its aim has always been to establish an independent Kurdish state in South Eastern Turkey where much of the majority is Kurdish. But the Kurd ethnic group is also spread across Iran, Iraq, Syria and countries of the former Soviet Union. At various times in their history, the Kurds have been subjugated by a combination of all these different countries as well as continually being let down by politicians in the West who have promised a homeland in return for military action. The largest grouping of Kurds is in Turkey, some 19 million people, around 28% of the country. In total across these countries there are around 36 million Kurds. Demographic estimates claim Kurds will make up almost half of the population of Turkey by 2050. The PKK has combined rural based attacks with those on the urban population as well. In an attempt to damage Turkey's tourist industry, it bombed tourist sites and hotels and kidnapped foreign tourists in the early-to-mid-1990s. Its main focus though has been on targeting Turkish diplomatic and security forces throughout Turkey and Western Europe. After the capture of Ocalan, in Kenya, he subsequently announced a peace plan and ordered members to refrain from violence; the Turkish State Security Court subsequently sentenced him to death. In January 2000, KWP members supported Ocalan's initiative and claimed the group now would use only political means to achieve its new goal, improved rights for Kurds in Turkey. This has largely been upheld. It has thousands of supporters throughout Turkey, Iraq and Europe. By April 2002 the group decided to change its name. It is now known as the Congress for Freedom and Democracy in Kurdistan and wants to campaign peacefully for Kurdish rights. The new group's aim is 'Democracy for Turkey and freedom for the Kurds. Federalism for Iraq and freedom for the Kurds. Democracy for Iran and freedom for the Kurds.'

REVOLUTIONARY PEOPLE'S LIBERATION PARTY

This group has been in existence since the late 1970s and has also been known as Devrimci Sol (Revolutionary Left) and Dev Sol. Virulently anti-Western and particularly anti-NATO and American it has maintained a political presence throughout Turkish life for the past 25 years. It rose to prominence in the 1980s when it began attacking Turkish security and military officials. By 1990 it also began a campaign against foreign interests. Then, it assassinated two US military contractors and wounded a US Air Force officer to protest against the Gulf War. In 1992 it launched a rocket attack against the US Consulate building in Istanbul. It has also assassinated prominent Turkish businessmen. In 2001 it conducted its first suicide bombings, targeting Turkish police, though the authorities have fought back arresting a number of leaders in the past few years severely weakening its position, although the RPLP still remains operational. It is thought to raise funds throughout Western Europe.

JAPANESE RED ARMY

This group was also known as the Anti-Imperialist International Brigade. It was formed in 1970 after breaking away from Japanese Communist League-Red Army Faction. It was led for 30 years by Fusako Shigenobu until her arrest in Japan in November 2000. After her arrest Shigenobu announced she intended to pursue her goals using party politics rather than violence. Its goal has always been to overthrow the Japanese Government and monarchy and, at the same time, help bring about a world revolution. Its base is in Japan but it also thought to have attempted to establish political cells in Singapore. It also has a history of close ties with Palestinian groups. Throughout the 1970s it conducted attacks around the world. In 1972, it carried out a massacre at Lod Airport in Israel, it hijacked two Japanese airliners and also tried to take over the US Embassy in Kuala Lumpur. Some of its members are in jail in the United States after a foiled attack. It is thought to have around six members currently still active and they are thought to be in the Middle East, possibly Syria.

EUROPE

Prior to 11 September, the fear of further terrorist attacks came not from al-Qaeda but from a range of groups pushing a nationalist agenda such as the Irish Republican Army and ETA as well as left-wing groups such as the Red Brigade, the Baader-Meinhof gang and November 17. Not all of these threats have gone away. They may not top the current political agenda but it is not long since they were top of terrorism's 'most wanted' list.

BASQUE FATHERLAND AND LIBERTY (ETA)

Basque Fatherland and Liberty is the English translation of Euskadi ta Askatasuna (ETA). It is a group formed in the northern parts of Spain – between the Spanish and French borders: the Basque country is not limited to Spain – which has long been trying to establish an independent Basque state. Their claims have been bitterly opposed by a succession of Spanish governments, though the Spanish constitution allows for a great deal of autonomy, with the Basque regional government having the freedom to set taxes and having responsibility for education, health care and policing among other things. This limited autonomy though is not enough for ETA. Their demands for separation from the Spanish state comes via Basque history. The Basques are a group which are linguistically and culturally separate from the rest of Spain. Their ancestors in the region can be traced back to the Stone Age. Despite this the Basques have never had their own independent state. Around two million people live in the region.

The armed struggle has been going on for five decades. For much of the time the focus of ETA's struggle has been Spanish government institutions and high-ranking officials. The group was formed in 1959 in protest at the oppression of the Franco regime, though it has to be said that this treatment was not only reserved for the Basques. It was in 1962 that ETA first took up arms however through the 1960s and the very early part of the 1970s its activities were relatively limited. This changed in 1973 when it killed the apparent successor to the dictatorship of General Franco, Admiral Luis Carrero Blanco using a bomb in the Madrid underground car park he regularly used. After 1975 and the death of Franco, ETA increasingly used violence as a political tool. The years 1979 and 1980 were very violent with around 130 deaths being attributed to the group.

Throughout the time of its fight with Madrid there have been an estimated 500 assassinations, 1,000 injuries and 60 kidnappings. Also targeted have been Basque industrialists. Around 100 ETA members have been killed, 20,000 have been arrested and around 600 are currently thought to be in prison. As well as the attack on Luis Carrero Blanco, ETA has tried to kill Jose Maria Aznar, the current leader of Spain, though the 1995 attack happened when he was in opposition. A plot to kill King Juan Carlos in the same year was foiled. There seemed to be hope that violence could be ended when a ceasefire was arranged in 1999. However this has since been broken. In November 2001 a judge and two police officers were killed. In March 2002 a local councilor was assassinated. This came just a few months after a French Gendarme was shot. This was highly unusual, as ETA has always been careful not to extend its struggle into France.

BAADER-MEINHOF GANG/RED ARMY FACTION

This group is probably one of the most well known terrorist groups, at least in Europe and formed part of a general fear of a terrorist future even way back in the 1970s. Baader-Meinhof seemed to capture the imagination of the public throughout the 1970s. This may have been because one of its leaders was female: terrorism has rarely been an area of equal opportunities. Whatever the reason, the group was able to leave its imprint on the volatile political scene of the 1970s.

Baader-Meinhof originated from three separate groups prominent in left-wing politics in West Germany in the late 1960s and the early 1970s. The three groups were known as the Red Army Faction (RAF), Movement 2 June and the Revolutionary Cells. Of these the RAF was the most-well known and it was also used by some as the name applied to Baader-Meinhof. The ideology of the group was a combination of Marxism and Maoism if you wish to be generous, or a spoilt middle-class rejectionism if you do not. Their appearance coincided with the most tumultuous time in West German politics. The student movement in Germany was the most radical in Europe at the time, outside France, and some of those involved in the leading student groups at the time went on to form Germany's radical Green group which is now part of Germany's government. Baader-Meinhof, though, followed the path of armed struggle.

In April 1968 Andreas Baader and his girlfriend Gudrun Enslinn firebombed the apartment of Frankfurt's Kaufhaus Schneider department store. Not a particularly significant act in itself but it set off a chain of events that proved to be so. Baader and Enslinn were convicted and jailed for the attack but escaped police custody in 1970 when Ulrike Meinhof, a left-wing journalist helped them escape. For the next two years these three plus Jan Carl Raspe and Holger Meins were on the run during which time they robbed banks and bombed buildings. This ended in a spectacular shootout on June 1, 1972 when Baader (along with Raspe and Meins) was captured by the West German police, again in Frankfurt. Baader was to spend the next four years in prison being tried and convicted in the most expensive trial in West German history. Baader died in prison in November 1977. He was either killed or committed suicide depending on your viewpoint. Ulrike Meinhof was captured on June 15, 1972 and spent the next four years in prison. On May 9, 1976, she hung herself in her cell though again the explanation of suicide has failed to satisfy some. Enslinn and Raspe died on the same day as Baader and it became known in West Germany as 'Death Night'. How they died once again depends on your viewpoint but the official verdict was suicide. Meins had died in 1974 on hunger strike. Baader-Meinhof could hold a record for being the only wrongly-named terrorist group in history. It implied that Meinhof was a co-leader of the group, which she was not, or that she was a lover of Baader's. Again, she was not. Indeed, Baader and Meinhof used to refer to their group as the Red Army Faction. The RAF has continued the struggle of Baader-Meinhof despite the arrest of many of its leaders over the years. In 1993 it bombed and destroyed a new prison and a police shootout ended with the death of one member, Wolfgang Grams, and one policeman. During the Gulf War it peppered the US Embassy in Bonn with shots from an assault rifle. There were no casualties. It is thought to have up to 20 members currently. It is self-financing though in the past it received money from East Germany and the Middle East.

One bizarre footnote: November 2002 saw the attempted return of the brain of Ulrike Meinhof by the German authorities to her family. Her daughter, Bettina Roehl, had filed a lawsuit demanding the return of her mother's brain, so that it could be given a proper burial. The brain had not been buried with the rest of the body but preserved for research and kept at Magdeburg University Hospital in eastern Germany.

NOVEMBER 17

In all of terrorism's history there has probably never been a group that has gone from being a seemingly untouchable secret operation to disappearing quite so fast as November 17. When it carried out an attack in June 2000 killing a UK defence attaché Stephen Saunders, very little was known about the group even though it had been in existence since 1975. By the time you read this, the group no longer exists. The group took its name from the date of a student uprising in 1973 when the then ruling Greek army killed 20 students. Its first attack was in December 1975 when it shot dead Richard Welch a Central Intelligence Agency chief based in Athens, as he returned from a party. The .45-calibre pistol used in the attack became the hallmark of the group's assassinations. The attack was carried out because of US support for the Greek military regime. Over the next 15 years November 17 would carry out 21 killings, including four US diplomats. The theme of all their attacks seemed to be anti-Western and aimed at ending military ties with the US. It was also firmly anti-capitalist and has called for an uprising at home. Other attacks include the killing of a former state bank governor in 1994 and a UK shipping tycoon in 1997. The murder of Saunders really brought the group to prominence in the UK.

Hopes that November 17 group would be stopped before they acted again seemed remote at best. However, in July 2002 the Greek authorities scored their first success against the group, which subsequently unravelled within a few months to leave the group virtually extinct. Savas Xiros was detained after the bomb he was trying to plant exploded. His fingerprints matched those found at another crime scene and from there the police were able to piece together details of the group. Just weeks later arrests of leaders of the group took place. By late summer the group had been decimated. The arrests were a big coup for the Greek authorities considering that the Olympics take place in Athens in 2004. Though we do not have the space to go into the subject here, how big a coup it could really be considered must be set against the fact that in retrospect the actions and planning of November 17 seem almost comical including false moustaches put on upside-down and so on.

THE IRISH REPUBLICAN ARMY

'The trouble with the Irish is the English.'

Anonymous Irish wit

If you ask almost anybody in the UK to name a terrorist group then it would not be al-Qaeda, instead it would be the Provos, the Provisional Irish Republican Army. The group has seared itself into the political consciousness over a 30-year or so terror campaign aimed at ending London's rule of Northern Ireland and bringing about a united isle with Dublin as the political center.

The struggle for political control of Northern Ireland's future has come at significant human cost. By the beginning of this century 3,500 people had been killed and 30,000 had been injured. When you consider that only just over 1.6 million people live in Northern Ireland that is a huge toll. The IRA (Oglaigh nah Eireann) was formed in 1919 as a commando unit opposed to the British, though its origins can be traced back to the Easter Rising of 1916. (Actually, the 'Irish problem' – or looked at differently the 'English problem' – can be traced back much further, as we have seen in Chapter 2). After the Irish Free State was established in 1922 the organization split. But although many remained disaffected by continued rule from London political violence was rare.

The 1960s changed this. Picking up on social unrest elsewhere civil liberties had become an issue within Northern
Ireland, along with the injustices, perceived and actual, that con-
fronted the minority Catholic population when it came to many
everyday things such as housing and jobs. By 1969 a new kind of
radicalism was rife, and a committed desire among many to try
and shape the destiny of Northern Ireland themselves had
become apparent. Left wing in origin, the IRA was intent on
getting British troops out of Northern Ireland. It has attempted
to do this through a variety of methods including bombings
both in Northern Ireland and mainland Britain, assassinations
including that of Earl of Mountbatten and the MP Airey Neave,
kidnappings, punishment beatings, extortion, and robberies.
Targets have generally included senior British Government officials, British military and police in Northern Ireland, and
Northern Irish Loyalist paramilitary groups such as the UVF.
Bombing campaigns have been conducted against economic
targets and a British military facility on the European continent.
If its aim was to get rid of the Brits then at present it is clear that
the policy has failed. However, it is clear that the group's
struggle has forced politicians in London to conduct negotia-
tions, in secret at first, but openly later in the knowledge that the
war in Northern Ireland cannot be won. The first talks achieved
a ceasefire between September 1994 and February 1996 though
this was broken with the bombing of Canary Wharf. However
since July 1997 it has observed a second ceasefire though opponents point to the fact that punishment beatings continue in
Northern Ireland itself. The violence has spawned a new political arrangement in Northern Ireland with autonomous
government now in place and much of Northern Ireland's deci-
sions taking place direct from Stormont. In the government are

members of Sinn Fein, the political wing of the IRA.

However in 2002 this was suspended for an alleged spying scandal within the heart of the Northern Ireland government. In October 2001, the IRA put a large number of its weapons beyond use but it is clear that should it want to it remains fully operative. It has defied calls for it to disarm totally. It is still thought to have several hundred members who operate in a highly organized cell-like structure. In the past it has received funding from groups in the US Irish community, the Palestinian Liberation Organization and Libya.

IRISH LOYALIST PARAMILITARY GROUPS

The IRA is not the only terrorist group in Northern Ireland – far from it. Loyalist groups, those that want to remain part of the United Kingdom and are made up of supporters from the majority Protestant community, have also played a large part in the troubles. Two main groups have carried out violent acts – the Ulster Volunteer Force and the Ulster Defence Association, also known as the Ulster Freedom Fighters. It is calculated that 30% of all deaths over the period of conflict within Northern Ireland can be attributed to the Loyalist groups.

The UVF was formed in 1966 and UDA in 1971. The groups have co-operated during the struggle in Northern Ireland though a bitter turf war erupted between supporters of both groups in 2001. The most significant of the attacks carried out by Loyalists include the first major act of sectarian violence in 1966 when four Catholics were murdered. They have also been responsible for the 1969 bombing of a power station near Belfast, the death of 33 civilians in Dublin and Monaghan in May 1974 through the use of bombs and the murder of Sinn Fein leader Gerry Adams' nephew in January 1998. While the IRA has largely concentrated on military and political targets, the Loyalist forces have tended to kill more out of religious hatred.

FRONTE DI LIBERAZIONE NAZIUNALE DI A CORSICA/ FRONT DE LIBERATION NATIONALE DE LA CORSE

The FLNC was founded in 1976 and has had a turbulent history marked by in-fighting and splits. Although several new groups peeled off the main structure, they have returned and the group is again the leading Corsican terror group, though others remain (see glossary). The FLNC was itself a product of a merger between two organizations, Ghjustizia Paolina and the Fronte Paesanu Corsu di Liberazione. Its underpinning ideology is the desire for an independent homeland for Corsica free from French rule. It is closely linked to a political party, A Cuncolta Independentista, which is considered as its legal representative. A Cuncolta is the only nationalist party with a delegation in the Corsican Assembly. Most of the attacks it has carried out have been in Corsica but some have also struck on mainland France. Historically they have been aimed at public infrastructure, banks, police buildings and tourist facilities. Throughout the 1990s the attacks became more violent culminating in the death in 1998 of Claude Erignac, the highest representative of the French Republic on the island. Later though the FLNC denied carrying out the attack. The total number of casualties since the group(s) began its action is around 220. The group is currently around 600 strong.

SOUTH AMERICA

SENDERO LUMINOSO (SHINING PATH)

This group rose to international prominence in the 1980s when it emerged as one of the most ruthless terrorist groups in the world. Up to 30,000 people are thought to have died since the group began its armed struggle to destroy Peruvian political institutions and replace them with a Maoist communist regime, although it should be noted that the Peruvian military have also been completely ruthless in their 'counter-terrorism' too.

Throughout the 1980s and 1990s terrorist attacks seemed to occur almost daily. The organization was set up by a university professor Abimael Guzman in the late 1960s. Sendero is strongly opposed to the outside influence of other countries in Peruvian affairs and also opposes any interference from other terrorist groups (see Tupac Amaru Revolutionary Movement). Shining Path considers itself the only true revolutionary movement in Peru. Its members have fought Tupac Amaru members in turf wars in remote parts of Peru.

In recent years several members of its leadership have been arrested undermining its influence. After taking up the armed struggle in 1980, it has conducted indiscriminate bombing campaigns as well as selective assassinations. In 1990 it attempted to car bomb the US embassy in Lima. Its membership has now dwindled to around 200 armed protagonists and it operates mostly in rural areas. This is largely because of a crackdown by disgraced former President Alberto Fujimori who upon winning an election in 1992 assumed quasi-dictatorial powers, abandoned the courts and used the military to take on Shining Path. It was a tactic with some success as many leaders were arrested. However a car bomb attack in March 2002 close to the US Embassy in Lima suggested that the potential for attacks still remain. The attack happened just before President Bush became the first US leader to visit Peru.

The ruthless violence of Sendero Luminoso is totally unjustified by any standards. However, as with other terrorist groups to say it is unjustified does not mean that it is inexplicable. The grinding poverty and exploitation associated with life in rural Peru and Sendero's simple message of revolution did, in the past, make it highly effective in recruiting simple peasants – both men and women – to take up arms in support of its aims.

TUPAC AMARU REVOLUTIONARY MOVEMENT

A left-wing revolutionary group which was established in 1983. It was formed from the remnants of another Peruvian group known as the Movement of the Revolutionary Left. Its aim is to establish a left-wing regime and rid Peru of all outside influence especially US and Japanese influence – Peru has a large Japanese ethnic community and a former president Fujimori who has fled to Japan following sleaze and corruption allegations. Like Sendero Luminoso its power to operate has been diminished in the past few years by the authorities imprisoning or killing many of its leaders and in fighting. It has conducted bombings, kidnappings, ambushes, and assassinations, and its most notable action was in December 1996 when 14 of its members occupied the Japanese Ambassador's residence in Lima. It held 72 people hostage for more than four months. All 14 members were killed when Peruvian forces stormed the residence in April 1997. One hostage also died. Since that time the group has not conducted a significant terrorist operation and seems to be more preoccupied with trying to get its members out of jail. Nowadays it is thought to have around 100 members.

FUERZAS ARMADAS REVOLUCIONARIOS DE COLUMBIA (REVOLUTIONARY ARMED FORCES OF COLOMBIA)

This group was set up in 1964, or 1966, depending on who you believe, as the military wing of the Colombian Communist Party. It is one of the most established terror groups in the country. Its activities include bombings, murders, kidnapping and hijacking and has largely been aimed at political, economic and military targets. US sources have been keen to talk up its well-established links with drug traffickers in the region. However, it is probably more accurate to say that the Colombian military, the government, and the United States – all of whom are more thoroughly implicated in the drugs trade – have used the drugs argument as an excuse to use whatever methods necessary to try and exterminate the FARC. The FARC themselves have always taken an anti-drug position except insofar as taxes on drug production have helped fund their operations. The group is probably made up of around 10,000 armed followers and has many more supporters especially in rural areas where social deprivation is extremely high. It is thought to be a highly organized group with a well-established command structure. FARC operates mainly in Colombia, with occasional operations in Venezuela, Panama, and Ecuador.

AFRICA

ARMED ISLAMIC GROUP

This is a group that aims to overthrow the secular Algerian regime and replace it with an Islamic state. Hugely violent, it began its campaign in 1992 after the Algiers regime ignored the result of an election which the Islamic Salvation Front (FIS) – the largest Islamic party – won in December 1991. It has attacked civilians, journalists and foreigners and conducted a campaign of massacres. It has killed more than 100 expatriate people based in Algeria, used assassination and has seemed to favour the slitting of throats as a method of killing. In 1994 it hijacked an Air France flight to Algiers in December and conducted a series of bombings in France. There has been some speculation that much of the terror work that has been carried out in its name was, in fact, carried out by the Algerian government anxious to vilify Islamic groups in the country; a dangerous tactic if it is true but typical of conspiracy theories surrounding terrorism. It is believed to have around 200 members and Algiers has accused Iran and Sudan of backing the group financially.

AFRICAN NATIONAL CONGRESS

There is a country in the world where terrorists were so successful that after a long armed struggle they eventually took over as rulers of the nation.

Indeed, they were so successful that they not only become rulers but also have been re-elected and are likely to remain in power for a long time given the extent of their support.

The country is South Africa and the terrorist group is the country's most powerful political party, the African National Congress (ANC), which was led for many years by the politician probably respected more than any other in the world, Nobel Peace Prize winner, Nelson Mandela.

To avoid putting the word terrorist in inverted commas, let's just remind ourselves – again - that 'one man's terrorist is... well you know how that sentence finishes by now.

However, despite his exalted reputation today, Mandela was for many a year considered nothing more than a terrorist.

The ANC was formed in 1912 in protest at the policies of the segregationist government of South Africa. Initially its resistance was non-violent and by the 1950s Nelson Mandela had become a prominent member of the Youth League Branch of the ANC. Its non-violent approach was to change, however, in 1960 after the Sharpeville massacre.

Protesting against a new law, which restricted the movement of black workers in white areas, the demonstration was brutally put down by the authorities with 70 people being killed. Immediately the protest movement against the Apartheid regime of South Africa – where whites ruled a country despite only accounting for around 13% of the total population – underwent a massive transformation.

The ANC and others were pushed underground as they were outlawed and they now took up armed struggle against the regime. The ANC formed the *Umkhonto we Sizwe* (Spear of the Nation) in direct response to a call for armed action.

Mandela advocated a course of 'non-terrorist' action largely aimed at the institutions of the state and provoking civil unrest. He was arrested in 1964 and sentenced to life imprisonment on charges of 'incitement to sabotage, treason and violent conspiracy'. Convicted – of which outcome there had been little doubt – he would spend the next 26 years in prison. Outside, the struggle against the racist regime was to get more violent. The brutal rule of the regime used tactics such as death squads to enforce its rule and the enmity between different black factions such as the ANC and Inkatha Freedom Party costs thousands of lives: how many, exactly, it is almost impossible to calculate.

In 1976 the black suburbs of Johannesburg, Soweto, rebelled in one of the most direct and open moments of opposition to white rule. Those opposed to the regime were strict in dealing with collaborators, the most well-known punishment being the 'necklace' – a tyre soaked with petrol, placed around a person's neck and set alight.

'With that stick of matches, with our necklace, we shall liberate this country,' said Nelson's former wife Winnie Madikizela Mandela in 1986.

Despite increasing international opposition to the South African regime, the government was propped up by powerful international supporters: during the Reagan era, for example, around 400 US companies had business interests in South Africa. UK business interests were also well represented and during her term in office the British Prime Minister Margaret Thatcher resisted calls for an economic and political boycott of the country. However as international pressure increased against the regime, the South African economy began faltering.

The US Congress eventually lifted the veto on sanctions against South Africa imposed by Ronald Reagan and many businesses soon saw that it was not within their interests to remain propping up a regime so universally loathed.

By 1990 the writing was on the wall for the racist South African government.

Nelson Mandela, the terrorist, was released in February of that year and at long last the ban on the ANC was lifted.

In May 1990 Mandela agreed to an end to the violent armed struggle.

In April 1994 the first multi-racial elections in South African history took place with the ANC polling 63% of the vote. Mandela became South Africa's first black president.

MINOR GROUPS

This section does not seek to be exhaustive and the borderline between terror and violent direct action is difficult to draw at times. In recent times attacks on establishments known to be frequented by homosexuals have been perpetrated by less organized forces than those which would be called terrorists. Racist attacks remain common and linked to far-right groups. Groups such as the Lesbian Avengers have engaged in sabotage. Feminists and other groups have taken 'direct action' against the pornography industry. Many societies are characterized by a whole range of situations in which violence is involved. For this reason we have excluded the arson of Welsh nationalists and the Scottish National Liberation Army; we suspect we are only aware of such things because of where we live and that groups as small as these have their equivalents the world over.

Britain's only home-grown terrorist group was called the Angry Brigade. They operated in the 1960s and 1970s and bombed the homes of establishment figures. In total 25 attacks were carried out between 1967 and 1971. Subsequently the group has apologized for its actions. Sticking with Britain, the 'Irish problem' has involved a whole range of splinter and smaller groups than those mentioned earlier. The INLA, or Irish National Liberation Army is a smaller group with similar aims to the IRA. The Continuity Irish Republican Army is a splinter group from the IRA which targets British military interests. Meanwhile the so-called Real IRA was formed in early 1998 as an armed wing of the 32-County Sovereignty Movement, a group dedicated to removing British forces from Northern Ireland and unifying Ireland. (See section on Omagh bombing, Chapter 4). Resembling though not as amusing as the 'splitters' in Monty Python's 'Life of Brian' in many situations where terrorist groups have emerged there also exist many smaller offshoots or linked groups. This suggests that where there is a cause for terrorism it will not always be unitary; the reasons for resentment may inspire a number of reactions. Getting the IRA to disarm still leaves smaller groups and the resentment which caused the IRA in the first place. Many of the following examples fit the pattern of smaller groups with similar aims to more famous bigger groups.

Al-Aqsa Martyrs Brigade

Aims to drive Israeli troops and settlers out of the West Bank, the Gaza Strip and Jerusalem and establish a Palestinian state. The first suicide bombing ever carried out by a female was for this group in January 2002.

Al-Gamaa al-Islamiyyah

See section on Luxor, Chapter 4.

Armata Corsa

Founded in 1999. It claims to act against the growing link between nationalist groups and the Mafia in Corsica. Considered a rival to the FLNC.

Armée Revolutionnaire Bretonne

A small terrorist group striving for an independent Brittany.

Asbat al-Ansar

It means the Partisans' League and is a Sunni Muslim group with links to bin Laden. It justifies violence against civilians and has championed the overthrow of the Lebanese government.

Lashkar-e-Tayyiba (Army of the Righteous)

Armed wing of the Pakistan-based religious organisation. Anti-US. The group was banned and its assets were frozen by the Pakistani Government in January 2002.

Mujahedin-e Khalq Organization

Marxist and Islamic group, apparently, formed in the 1960s. It has attacked Iranian embassies.

National Liberation Army (ELN)

Colombian group formed in 1965 inspired by the Cuban revolution. 5,000 armed followers relied on kidnapping, hijacking and bombing.

Palestine Islamic Jihad

Group that started in the Gaza Strip in the 1970s. Wants the creation of an Islamic Palestinian State

Revolutionary Nuclei

Greek group that is anti-US/NATO/European Union. Bombing and arson attacks were its hallmark. Nothing reported since 2000.

The Salafist Group for Call and Combat

Splinter group from the GIA that has gained popular support among Algerians despite civilians being attacked. Most targets are military.

United Self-Defence Forces/Group of Colombia

Formed in April 1997 to consolidate local and regional paramilitary groups and to protect economic interests. Linked to drug trafficking, the military and thence to US forces. Over 8,000 strong.

15 May Organization

Formed in 1979 and claimed responsibility for several bombings in the early-to-middle 1980s including a hotel bombing in London in 1980.

Alex Boncayao Brigade

A hit squad affiliated to the Communist Party of the Philippines New People's Army. Largely attacked governmental targets.

Armenian Secret Army for the Liberation of Armenia

Not so secret, as it turns out. Formed in 1975. Wants Turkish government to acknowledge publicly the deaths of 1.5 million Armenians in 1915 and cede territory for Armenian homeland.

Army for the Liberation of Rwanda

Murderous group that carried out the Rwandan Hutu genocide of 500,000 in East Africa in 1994. Wants to topple Tutsi-dominated government.

Chukaku-Ha

A left wing Japanese group dating back to 1957 that formed out of the country's Communist Party. Opposed to Western imperialism.

Democratic Front for the Liberation of Palestine

Founded in 1969 and believes Palestinian national goals can be achieved only through revolution of the masses.

Sipah-e-Sahaba Pakistan

Its name means Guardian of the Friends of the Prophet and the group has been alleged to be involved in terrorist attacks against the Shia community in Pakistan.

GRAPO

Formed in 1975 as the armed wing of the illegal Communist Party of Spain. Advocates the overthrow of the Spanish Government. Has killed more than 80 people.

Force 17

Formed in early 1970s as a personal security force for Yasser Arafat. In September 1985 it claimed responsibility for killing three Israelis in Cyprus.

Jabhat al-Kifah al-Sha'bi/ Palestinian Popular Struggle Front

Established before the Six Day War of 1967 in the West Bank. It has close links to Al-Fatah. Has intermittently fallen out with the PLO over tactics towards Israel. Terrorist attacks included killing a child in an attack on an El Al building in Athens in 1969.

Jamaat ul-Fuqra

Islamic group that calls for the purification of Islam through violence.

Lautaro Youth Movement

Advocates the overthrow of the Chilean Government. Became active in late 1980s, but has been weakened in recent years.

Loyalist Volunteer Force

Formed in 1996 as a faction of the Ulster Volunteer Force. Attacked Catholic politicians, civilians, and Protestant politicians who endorsed the Northern Ireland peace process.

Manuel Rodriguez Patriotic Front

Founded in 1983 as the armed wing of the Chilean Communist

Party. Named after the hero of Chile's war of independence against Spain. Attacked US businesses.

Morazanist Patriotic Front

A group that first appeared in the late 1980s protesting against US intervention in Honduran politics. Probably considered 'terrorist' because it failed to grow to reach the 'guerrilla' status of the FMLN in neighbouring El Salvador.

National Liberation Army

Claims to be a group set up by Che Guevara. Has attacked US interests in Bolivia.

New People's Army

Military wing of the Communist Party of the Philippines. Opposes US interests in the country.

People Against Gangsterism and Drugs

Formed in 1996 as a community anticrime group fighting drugs and violence in Cape Town. However by 1998 had become anti-government, anti-Western and Islamic.

Popular Front for the Liberation of Palestine-Special Command:

Claimed responsibility for several attacks in Western Europe, including the bombing of a restaurant frequented by US servicemen in Torrejon, Spain, in April 1985. Eighteen Spanish killed in the attack.

Popular Struggle Front

Palestinian group that led attacks against Israeli, moderate Arab, and PLO targets.

Puka Inti

Anti-US Ecuadorian group with fewer than 50 members

Red Brigade

A left-wing group that left its mark on European politics in the 1970s and 1980s. It arose from the student protest movement and attacked members of the establishment in its class struggle. Also demanded Italian withdrawal from NATO. Declined in the 1980s and its leaders renounced violence.

Red Hand Defenders

Protestant hard-line group credited with killing Irish human rights lawyer Rosemary Nelson.

Revolutionary People's Struggle

Group opposed to Western influence in Greece. Formed in 1971. Attacked governmental targets.

Revolutionary United Front

Group seeking to topple the government of Sierra Leone and to retain control of the lucrative diamond-producing regions of the country.

Tupac Katari Guerrilla Army

Anti-Western Bolivian group that has attacked pipelines, power pylons and Mormon churches.

Al Ummah

Indian Muslim group founded in 1992 responsible for bombings in southern India.

Zviadists

Supporters of former Georgian President Zviad Gamsakhurdia who launched a revolt against his successor, Eduard Shevard-nadze, which was suppressed in late 1993. Two assassination attempts against Shevardnadze.

This list does not even get close to including all the groups which existed but which now do not (such as the Mau Mau in Kenya) and fails to include some major right wing death squads and left-wing guerrilla groups. However, it does begin to give some idea of the variety of people prepared to use violence, and the variety of causes that inspire them to do so. As weapons have become more available and violence has spread, the state response has often been more deadly than the terror. Indeed state violence has often given rise to terrorism. It is to these topics that we now turn.

4 TERROR ATTACKS AROUND THE GLOBE

MUNICH, 05.09.1972: MASSACRE AT THE OLYMPICS

The murder of 11 Israeli athletes at the Munich Olympics in September 1972 remains one of the most infamous terrorist attacks in history. It is also one of the most bizarre tales of modern history, marked not only by tragedy but also staggering incompetence on the part of the German authorities and revenge on the part of the Israeli government. And much of it was played out in front of the world's television cameras.

It was early on the morning of 5 September when the Israeli athletes' compound was entered by five Arab terrorists, from the pro-Palestinian Black September Organization. The five were dressed as athletes and although they were spotted on their way to the compound nobody thought they were anything other than competitors at the Games. The five were joined by three colleagues who had already entered the compound, probably with official accreditation. The initial operation was anything but smooth. The first victims – Moshe Weinberger, a wrestling coach, and Joseph Romano, a weightlifter – were killed almost immediately as the terrorists tried to round up Israeli athletes inside the compound. Weinberger's body was later dumped in the street. Nine more would be captured but not without a struggle. They also missed rounding up further athletes because of the fight the athletes put up. Some Israelis had also managed to escape the compound.

By breakfast time, the Palestinians announced that they had taken the Israelis hostage and in return demanded the release of 234 Arab and German prisoners held in Israel and West Germany, including members of the Baader-Meinhof gang (see pp. 84–86), who had been arrested earlier that year. They also demanded safe passage out of West Germany to Egypt for themselves. The Israeli athletes were to be released once the terrorists had reached their destination. The Israeli government refused to meet the demands of the terrorists and the Egyptian government would not allow the entry of the terrorists onto their soil.

The West German state authorities, in overall charge of the operation, decided that a rescue attempt was the only option. The event was highly embarrassing for the German authorities. The 1972 Olympics, quite apart from attracting the sort of prestige normally associated with the Games, was also an attempt by the West German state to restore its good name in the eyes of a world which still held all-too-clear memories of its recent Nazi past. It was also trying to erase the memory of the Nazi-dominated 1936 Berlin Olympics. With this recent past in mind, the fact that Israeli athletes had been captured made it even more embarrassing. Some have suggested that the reason the terrorists were able to take the athletes hostage was because of the general lax security, security that was lax precisely because the West German government wanted to show the world that it was a new, modern, Western-style democracy. Unfortunately farce began to creep in.

A plan to rescue the athletes using troops failed when it transpired that it was being filmed by television crews and watched on TV by the terrorists in the compound! Subsequently the

West German authorities decided to launch its rescue attempt, using sharpshooters, at Furstenfeldbruck Airport where the planes demanded for the terrorists' flight from the country were being held. The terrorists and hostages were transferred to the airport from the Olympic Village first by bus then by helicopter. The state authority refused to allow specially trained Sayeret troops to take part in the operation. However things began to go wrong early at the airport when the West German police discovered that there were in fact eight terrorists, three more than they were expecting. Unfortunately there were only five snipers. Eight further police officers were posing as flight attendants and crew near a dummy 727 plane set up by the authorities, but they were without radio contact. The terrorists and their captives had been transported to the airport, some 15 miles from Munich, by two helicopters. As the terrorists moved from the helicopters, with the athletes tied up inside, the West German police decided to pounce. During the ensuing gun battle, lasting one hour and 15 minutes, a grenade was tossed into one of the helicopters, killing five of the luckless athletes inside.

The four hostages in the second helicopter were shot dead. A later investigation by the West German police conceded some of the hostages might have inadvertently been shot dead by the police. During the battle the media were informed that the hostages had been freed. Five terrorists were also killed, three were captured and one policeman died. A month after this a Lufthansa jet was hijacked by terrorists demanding that the Munich killers be freed. The West German government agreed and the terrorists were returned home. Subsequently it has been discovered that the West German authorities were complicit in staging the hijacking of the Lufthansa plane.

The Israeli response to the events at the Olympics was swift.

A top secret Cabinet committee – Cabinet X – was convened by Prime Minster Golda Meir. It established a Mossad (Israeli secret service) team to avenge the attacks on the athletes. This team carried out, one by one, assassinations on those it thought involved in the events that September. At least 12 men were targeted by the Israeli authorities. Ten were killed by the Israelis and one died of natural causes. However, the man thought to be the mastermind behind the capture of the athletes, Abu Daoud, remains at large.

One bizarre footnote to the events was that the Olympic Games continued after a temporary suspension. It is easy to sympathise with the journalist who wrote: 'It's like having a dance at Dachau,'.

ROME, 16.03.1978: THE ASSASSINATION OF ALDO MORO

'It was necessary to kill today to live tomorrow,'

Red Brigade leader Renato Curci

The Italian terrorist group Red Brigade (Brigate Rosse) made headlines across the globe when it kidnapped and assassinated Aldo Moro, the country's foreign minister and a five-time Prime Minister, on 16 March, 1978. The audacious coup showed the extent to which terrorist groups could penetrate state structures.

Moro was a leading light in attempting to construct the 'compromesso storico' – historical compromise – between Italian communists and the Christian Democrat group of which Moro was a member. Tipped to be the next president of Italy, he had been central in the process of trying to form a government of 'national solidarity' incorporating members from across the political spectrum which attempted to deal with the grave economic and social problems faced by Italy at that time. In the national solidarity cabinet were to sit members of the Italian

Communist Party – the first time this had happened in the country's history. On the very day this government was to get parliamentary approval, a process known as the 'fiducia', Moro was kidnapped and his five-man bodyguard was murdered. Despite a nationwide manhunt for Moro – of which more later – for all of the 55 days he was kept as a prisoner by the Red Brigade, Moro was housed in an apartment in Rome the country's cultural and political heart.

During this time Moro wrote several letters to political leaders, Pope Paul VI (who ended up personally conducting Moro's funeral mass), United Nations General Secretary Kurt Waldheim and to his own family. It has been suggested that he tried to send cryptic messages to his family through these letters. However, the authorship of many of these letters has subsequently been called into dispute.

Originally, the Red Brigade's plan was to exchange Moro for captured colleagues who were facing trial. His abduction coincided with the arrest in Turin of Renato Curci, a Red Brigade leader and the man responsible for the quote above. Curci and others were to be tried in a cage in a court guarded by 8,000 armed police. The Italian government though, headed by President Giulio Andreotti (sentenced in November 2002 to 24 years in jail for his murder of a journalist), adopted a no-negotiation stance with the Red Brigade (for which it received unequivocal international support). Pictures of Moro sitting below a Brigate Rosse flag were distributed at the time of his incarceration and have become an enduring image of his capture, and the ultimate hopelessness of his situation.

During his incarceration he was tried by a Red Brigade 'people's court' and executed. His body was dumped in a car parked in a Rome side street at a site metres away from the headquarters of both the Italian Communist and Christian Democrat parties. That the Red Brigade was able to dump Moro's body at such a point despite widespread police surveillance at the time was a final snub to the police and state apparatus. Moro was killed on May 9, 1978. He was 61 years old.

Since his death, mystery has surrounded Moro's abduction and murder. There have been questions as to how such a prominent politician could have been snatched so easily, how he could have been hidden in Rome despite a whole country looking for him and house searches carried out of known figures on the left and if some politicians knew more than they were letting on and who was ultimately responsible for his death. Conspiracy theorists (them again!) have pointed the finger at P2, an Italian Masonic lodge, for orchestrating Moro's murder. Others have looked in the direction of the US intelligence agencies. They claim that Moro's support for allowing the Communist Party into the echelons of power frightened the Americans. Certainly the CIA's own records point to the fact that they tried to keep the communists out of power in the immediate post-war period and throughout the 1960s and 1970s. During the Cold War the threat of Italy 'going red' was ever present. One theory has it that the Red Brigade had been substantially infiltrated by the CIA, though none of this has ever been proven.

There is also no need to look outside Italy for those who had motives to remove Moro from power. At a massively turbulent time in Italian politics, Moro was suggesting putting into place a radical proposal which would have altered the political status quo in Italy and threatened the power of ruling interest groups, specifically the Christian Democrat party. Questions have also been asked about who actually knew where Moro was during his capture and several politicians known to have been opposed to the plans to include the communists in a cabinet have been accused of knowing exactly where Moro was. Several inquiries have taken place into the whole affair but have failed to answer many questions. They remain unanswered 25 years later. The one indisputable fact was that Moro was kidnapped and murdered. And despite his central role in Italian post-war politics during his life he is remembered more for the manner of his death.

Whether the Moro affair was beneficial for highlighting the causes of the Red Brigade is highly debatable as well. Italians had become increasingly cynical about their politicians and the mystery that surrounded the whole affair seemed to add to that cynicism. There was also very little sympathy for the Red Brigade and its methods. During the Moro affair they violently attacked other Christian Democrat leaders and even kneecapped one politician based in Rome. Any support they may have hoped to garner from the public was lost with the Moro affair. By the 1980s the Red Brigade had become increasingly marginalized and many of their leaders had renounced the armed struggle.

IRAN, 04.11.1979: HOSTAGE CRISIS IN THE DESERT

'Let terrorists be aware that when the rules of international behaviour are violated, our policy will be one of swift and effective retribution. We hear it said that we live in an era of limit to our powers. Well, let it also be understood, there are limits to our patience.'

Ronald Reagan, January 1981,
on the release of the American hostages from Iran

On the morning of 4 November 1979, 3,000 pro-Ayatollah Khomeini students stormed the compound of the United States embassy in Tehran and took staff hostage. Student leaders would hold 52 people hostage for the next 444 days, until the White House had seen a change of leader, showing the limits to the influence of the world's most powerful country, and plunging relations between the two countries to a new low. Even today, this event continues to sour US-Iranian relations: Washington last year announced that Iran was part of an 'Axis of Evil' that threatens the entire world as we know it.

Until 1979 relations between the two countries were more than cordial, and the United States' influence in Iran had been keenly felt. After using the country as an important supply route during the Second World War, Washington was keen to retain its influence on the country in the Cold War period. Iran, under its Prime Minister Mossadegh, was keen to lessen the influence of foreign powers but the USA through the work of the Central Intelligence Agency (CIA) was keen to keep Iran 'on side'. Through interference in internal politics they were successful in driving Mossadegh from power and putting in his place the pro-Western Shah of Iran. The ultimate price Washington had to pay was that when Iranians found out the extent of the CIA's involvement in getting rid of their Prime Minister a simmering resentment of the USA was fostered in Iran. By 1964, the Shah had passed a controversial law giving American military personnel serving in Iran the same immunity from Iranian law that all foreign diplomats enjoyed. The US's position in Iran was assured.

One of the most outspoken critics of the Shah regime was the Islamic leader Ayatollah Rhuollah Khomeini. He was sent into exile in November 1964 and fled to Turkey. As he went into exile he vowed to have his revenge on the Shah and the US. Unlike most threats this one was carried out.

By the 1970s, the resentment against the US-backed Shah

regime had grown. There were attacks on American military personnel. By 1978, Khomeini was in Paris and plotting the downfall of the regime. On January 16, 1979, the Shah (terminally ill it transpired with cancer) flew from Iran never to return. He sought refuge but this was denied and ended up in Egypt, Morocco and the Bahamas among other countries. With the Shah gone the Ayatollah returned to become the country's new leader. He cut off US access to Iranian oil and cancelled $7 billion of arms contracts. Anti-Americanism was rife and the eventual hostage crisis was the second time the US embassy had been stormed by revolutionary students.

U-turning on his decision not to allow the Shah into the United States, President Jimmy Carter allowed the Shah into the country in October 1979 for surgery. The effect in Iran was catastrophic. Thousands poured onto the streets demanding he be returned and with him his multi-million dollar fortune that Iranians claimed was theirs. The eventual taking of the hostages satiated the need for revenge in Tehran but also demonstrated to the USA the limits of what it could and could not do in various countries around the world. The sight of the blindfolded US Marines embassy guard being led in front of television cameras had a shocking effect.

By February 1980, the Ayatollah demanded that the Shah be returned to Iran to face trial and also wanted an admission of guilt from the USA for its actions previously in Iran. As a presidential election loomed and with political avenues seemingly exhausted, Carter turned to the military for a solution. On 24 April, 1980, eight helicopters were launched from the US aircraft carrier Nimitz off of the south east coast of Iran. Simultaneously, six transport aircraft took off to rendezvous with the helicopters in the Iranian desert. Their mission seemed a daring one to release hostages in Tehran. 'Operation Eagle Claw' as it was known turned out to be a disaster however and was misconceived from start to finish. Eight American servicemen were subsequently killed and no hostages freed. The event undermined Jimmy Carter's attempt to get re-elected as President. By July 1980 the Shah was dead. By September Iraq had invaded Iran embarking on a futile war. With America freezing Iranian assets and Tehran's need for military weaponry the hostage crisis was coming to a head. Republican candidate Ronald Reagan was worried that any resolution in the crisis would have led to the re-election of Carter. How much everybody was involved in bringing home the hostages to the USA is a little blurred as the Reagan camp had developed an extensive network with members of the American intelligence agencies looking into freeing the hostages.

On Jimmy Carter's last day in office Carter agreed to pay the Iranian government $8 million in assets that had been frozen in return for release of the hostages. They arrived back in the USA on the very day Ronald Reagan began his eight-year presidency, 20 January, 1981. The agreement gave Iran immunity from any future lawsuits but in 2000, former hostages and their survivors sued Iran under an act that allows US citizens to sue foreign governments in cases of state-sponsored terrorism. Although they won their case in 2002, the US State Department sought the dismissal of the suit because they claimed it would hinder the government in negotiating future international agreements. Even though all the main players have left the world stage (Khomeini dead, Reagan has Alzheimer's disease) relations between the two countries remain tense. The current US President, George W. Bush has named Iran as one of three countries that made up the 'axis of evil'. Tehran has criticized American arrogance for making such a claim. Both, interestingly are among the few countries world-wide where it is possible to execute minors.

BEIRUT, 18.04.1983: US EMBASSY BOMBING

In 1983, US interests in the Middle East came under sustained terrorist attack resulting in a huge loss of life. Three separate attacks occurred against United States' political and military institutions. All three were similar in their execution and all three were deadly in their outcome. On 18 April 1983, 63 people were killed, including the Central Intelligence Agency's entire Middle East contingent, when a suicide bomb hit the US embassy in Beirut, Lebanon. On 23 October 242 Americans were killed by a suicide truck bomber in an attack on a military compound in Beirut. At the same time 58 troops were killed in a similar attack on French barracks. On 12 December four more people were killed when a suicide truck bomb was driven into the compound of the US Embassy in Kuwait. In total, including the attack on the French base, 367 people were killed.

The attacks came at a heightened time of tension within international politics. Washington was controlled by the hawkish regime of Ronald Reagan. At the same time that American troops were being slaughtered in the Middle East, Reagan was preparing to send American servicemen and women into action in the Caribbean. The Cold War was still at its height; Mikhail Gorbachev would not become leader of the USSR for another two years. And in the Middle East, US relations with Iran were still at rock bottom following the relatively recent resolution of the hostage crisis (see below). In June 1982, Israel had invaded Lebanon by land, sea and air. Beirut, one of the most important capitals in the Arab world was virtually destroyed. Up to 8,000

Palestinians and Lebanese were held as prisoners, and Israeli troops eventually occupied Beirut. The Palestinian Liberation Organization only agreed to leave their positions in Beirut under international supervision including US troops. It was against such a tumultuous international background that the attacks on American personnel and institutions took place.

The April attack occurred when a truck loaded with a 2,000-pound suicide bomb was driven at high speed into the US Embassy compound tearing through a seven storey building. Many people died as the building collapsed on top of them. Seventeen of those killed were Americans, the rest a combination of 'foreign' staff and aid workers. Responsibility for the attack was claimed by Islamic Jihad, though this claim has been questioned by some sources. Many in Washington still believe that responsibility for the attack lies with Syria and Iran, both deeply anti-American at the time. American intelligence claims that information gathered shows that Hezbollah guerrillas working for both Syria and Iran carried out the attack and used Jihad as a cover for their work. The US claimed that any suicide bombers were offered entry into paradise for killing an enemy of Iran. Hezbollah, Syria and Iran all denied any involvement in the bombing.

The second attack occurred six months later in very similar circumstances. A truck loaded with 12,000 pounds of TNT explosives was driven into the US Marine headquarters in Beirut. On explosion 242 serviceman were killed. A further 80 were injured. The attack happened at the same time that the USA invaded the tiny island of Grenada, fearful of the spread of 'communism' in the Caribbean. Two minutes after the attack on the US garrison, another truck packed with explosives crashed into a French paratrooper base just two miles down the road. By the end of that attack 58 French servicemen had also been killed. Again, Islamic Jihad claimed responsibility for the attack: again, the US was suspicious and believed that the attack was carried out by Hezbollah for Iran and Syria. Within five months the USA said it had connected up to 13 individuals to the attack including Mohammed Hussein Fadlallah, the leader of the Iranian-backed Hezbollah group.

The first two attacks had set the tone for the third. Despite the increased security another US headquarters was hit just two months after the death of 242 American servicemen. Again, a truck laden with explosives crashed into the compound of the US Embassy annex in Kuwait City. Four people were killed and a further 62 were injured. Another six targets were attacked in Kuwait that day. Again the US links the attack to Hezbollah even though Jihad claimed responsibility. The Kuwaiti authorities' response was swift. Within a week of the attack, they rounded up 10 individuals believed to have ties with radical Islamic groups. By 1984 sixteen people would be convicted for the attack and were sent to jail. Six people were also sentenced to death. Despite this Islamic Jihad would claim responsibility for more attacks in the following years including the repeat bombing in September 1984 of the US Embassy in Beirut.

NEW DELHI, INDIA, 31.10.1984: INDIRA GANDHI ASSASSINATED

On 31 October 1984 the Indian Prime Minster Indira Gandhi left her house to visit the actor Peter Ustinov in New Delhi. She never made it and was instead gunned down by her two Sikh bodyguards. She was 66 years old. Despite several warnings that her life was in danger, Mrs Gandhi had ignored the threats preferring to believe they were nothing serious. It was a major miscalculation. In fact, her dismissal of the assassination threats was shown in her choice of bodyguard. Gandhi was considered, rightly it turned out, to be most at risk from India's Sikh community. They had wanted revenge for an incident that had occurred just months earlier – the storming of the Golden Temple of Amritsar, a holy Sikh site. Ever since the attack, Sikhs had vowed revenge. On 31 October they got it. However it sparked off vicious rioting which left many thousands of Sikhs – some calculations put it as high as 3,000 – dead at the hands of the majority Hindu population outraged at the killing of one of the most prominent leaders the country had ever had, and a member of India's ruling political dynasty.

Indira Priyadarshin Gandhi was born in 1917, the only child of Kamla and Jawaharlal Nehru. Her father was the first Prime Minister of India and Indira's upbringing was privileged. She was educated in Switzerland and at Oxford University. She spoke fluent French and claimed Joan of Arc to be her role model. Indira Gandhi worked her way towards the higher echelons of the ruling Congress Party and by the time of her father's death in 1964 was one of the most prominent figures in Indian political life. She was made Minister of Information in Lal Bahadur Shastri's government. When Shastri died of a heart attack in 1966, Gandhi became the country's first woman Prime minister. It was a surprise. She had not been expected to take over so soon after her father's death. But after colleagues had failed to choose a candidate she emerged as the compromise choice and one who at the time was seen as easily manipulable.

She proved anything but and remained as Prime Minister for the next nine years skillfully exploiting India's victory over Pakistan in the war of 1971 and bathing in the national pride of India developing the nuclear bomb in 1974. Her politics at first were considered 'socialist' as she set about aggressively nationalizing major industries in India and came to international prominence for her championing the cause of non-alignment towards Moscow and Washington at the height of the Cold War.

However, by the mid-1970s her government was beset by allegations of corruption, the economy was wobbling and living standards had failed to get better. There were demands for her resignation after the High Court of Allahabad found her guilty of using illegal practices to secure her victory during elections. She was ordered by the court in 1975 to leave office and not return to politics for six years. Her response was not to go quietly but instead to declare a state of emergency. Her heavy-handed style of politics was reflected by the work of her son Sanjay who became a hated figure for his removal of people from slum dwellings and a highly resented program of forced sterilization of the poorest in society. By 1977, with the Congress Party doing badly in the polls, she was forced from office and considered to be a spent force.

However, within three years she was back leading the country (in the same year her son Sanjay, her chosen heir, was killed in an air crash) and would do so up until her assassination. Her second term in office was marked by her efforts to try and resolve the political problems of the state of Punjab. This was the richest region in India and as well as its wealth it was marked by its religious differences particularly with its large Sikh population. Many Sikhs wanted to create the independent state of Khalistan. They were led by Jarnail Singh Bindranwale.

The Sikh political centre was the 'Golden Temple' of Amritsar, a fabled site in the Sikh religion. Mrs Gandhi though saw it as the centre for Bindranwale to direct his activities against the Indian State and wanted the site flushed out. In June 1984, she began 'Operation Blue Star', which sought to clamp down on Bindranwale once and for all. In an attack on the Golden Temple, the Sikh leader was killed but the temple was damaged, earning Mrs Gandhi the undying hatred of Sikhs across India. More than 600 people were killed in the attack on Amritsar. Months later she was assassinated because of Operation Blue Star. On her death her son Rajiv was installed as leader. He concluded peace talks with Sikh leaders but he too was to be assassinated – by Sri Lankan Tamil Tigers – in 1991. The death of Rajiv prompted many in the West to compare the fate of the Gandhis to the fate of the Kennedy family in the United States. His widow, the Italian-born Sonia Gandhi was later to apologize for the storming of Amritsar by her mother-in-law

22.06.1985: THE BOMBING OF AIR INDIA FLIGHT 182

On 22 June, 1985, 329 people were killed after a bomb placed on board Air India flight 182 from Toronto to Delhi, via London, exploded off the coast of the Republic of Ireland. The bomb exploded while the plane was flying at 31,000 feet. Amazingly some of the passengers on board survived the fall only to drown in the cold waters of the Atlantic. Ultimately there were no survivors. Eighty-two of those killed were children. The wreckage was scattered along a nine-mile swathe of the ocean at a depth of 6,000 feet. The cockpit voice recorder showed there had been a loud bang aboard the aircraft. It also picked up the hissing sound of the fuselage opening up and a scream. The data recorders showed everything was normal on the aircraft until the explosion.

At the time it was the deadliest terrorist aviation attack in history. The bomb was loaded onto the plane in a suitcase. In fact the death toll from the terrorist attack was higher than 329.

Two deadly cargoes were loaded at Vancouver on the same day, 22 June. One ended up aboard flight 182 and another blew up in Tokyo's Narita Airport, while being transferred to another Air India flight en route to Bangkok, killing two baggage handlers, Hideo Asano and Hideharu Koda. Authorities say the bag was supposed to blow up on board Air India Flight 301, which was waiting to take off from Tokyo for Bangkok. That explosion happened just 55 minutes before the one over the Atlantic Ocean. One theory has it that the bomb on board flight 182 was supposed to blow up after the Boeing 747 had landed in London and the passengers had disembarked. But the flight was delayed and the plane fell into the Atlantic Ocean some 150 miles southwest of Ireland

Most of those killed were from British Columbia's large Asian community. And despite the fact that many Canadians were killed the roots of the attack were in India. A year before an attack had taken place on the Sikh holy shrine, the Golden Temple in Amritsar (see previous section) and the Sikh group Babbar Khalsa was pressing its demands for an independent Sikh state, Khalistan, in Punjab. Translated, Babbar Khalsa means 'Tigers of the True Faith'. The organization was established in the late 1970s.

The attacks heralded the beginning of the longest and most expensive criminal investigation ever mounted by Canadian police. Some estimates reckon that the investigation has cost around $25 million (Canadian). In October 2000, two Sikhs, both from Canada, were arrested and charged in connection with the bombings. A third suspect has subsequently been charged. The investigation has been fraught with difficulties however, with accusations that it had been bungled from the very outset.

Just months before the attack the then Indian Prime Minister

Rajiv Ghandi, who himself would be assassinated, visited North America. There were security concerns surrounding the visit and the Indian government had made prior arrangements with their US and Canadian intelligence counterparts to monitor and clamp down on Sikh 'extremists' before the visit. This led to round the clock surveillance of several members of the Sikh community and allegations that the bomb plot could have been detected by police before the atrocity was committed. Some of those under surveillance were subsequently arrested – but later released – in the initial stages of the police inquiry. Evidence, particularly tape-recorded conversations of those under suspicion, was destroyed before it could be used.

During the time that the investigation has been meandering along other theories for responsibility for the attack have come into the public domain. One of these centered around the fact that the bombings were not carried out by Sikh groups but rather by the Indian government looking to discredit Sikh groups across the planet. This theory has it that the Indian government had given a substantial loan to Babbar Khalsa just before the attacks and that the Indian authorities were complicit in stalling the investigations once they were started. All such allegations were denied by the Indian government and, it has to be said, conspiracy theories emerge in relation to a great many terrorist attacks.

LOCKERBIE, 21.12.1988: PAN AM FLIGHT 103

On the night of 21 December, 1988, Pan Am flight 103 on route from Frankfurt to New York, via Heathrow, was blown out of the sky over the Scottish town of Lockerbie by a bomb placed on board. 270 were killed. This included all 259 people on board and 11 people on the ground. Among the dead were 189 Americans. The average age of those who died was under 35 and many were university students returning home to the States for the Christmas holidays. At the time it was the second worst ever case of airline terrorism. The impact of the plane crashing on the ground was so strong that it measured 1.6 on the Richter Scale. The part of the plane that fell on Lockerbie created a crater some 200 feet long and 150 feet wide. The flight was at 31,000 feet when it exploded: despite that, two passengers are believed to have survived the fall but died not long afterwards on the ground. It is reckoned the weight of the plane fragments that fell on Lockerbie was more than 1,500 tonnes. Following a long process of trying to find those responsible, Abdelbaset Ali Mohmed al-Megrahi, a Libyan, was found guilty of 270 murders at a specially convened Scottish court in Camp Zeist, Holland and jailed for life in January 2000. Currently he is incarcerated in Barlinnie Prison, Scotland. An appeal against the conviction failed in March 2002. Al-Megrahi continues to claim his innocence and is currently appealing against his conviction at the European Court of Human Rights. A second defendant, Al Ahmin Khalifa Fhima was acquitted of the same charges of mass murder.

These are the basic facts about the Lockerbie disaster. Much else about the terrorist attack is shrouded in mystery. Almost as soon as the plane came down theories have abounded about how much was known beforehand – especially by Western governments – and who was really responsible for planting the bomb. The whole issue is, as ever, a rich seam for conspiracy theorists.

First of all the incident happened just five months after the American warship the USS *Vincennes* 'accidentally' shot down an Iranian passenger plane, Iran Air Flight 655, flying over the

Persian Gulf killing all 290 passengers on board. Some of those on board were travelling to the Islamic holy city of Mecca. (The captain of the *Vincennes* was ultimately decorated by the US government with the Legion of Merit award for 'exceptionally meritorious conduct in the performance of an outstanding service'). In the weeks leading up to the Lockerbie disaster it was widely believed that the Iranian government was planning a revenge attack. Was Lockerbie that attack? A group known as the Popular Front for the Liberation of Palestine may have carried out the attack on behalf of Iran, or perhaps on behalf of other Middle Eastern governments that have sponsored terrorism, including Syria.

Certainly conspiracy theorists can point to who DID NOT board the plane as evidence that Western governments and their security services knew something was up. Several US government officials ended up not flying on Pan Am 103 despite being booked to do so. The US ambassador to Cyprus was also thought to have plans to take the flight. And Pik Botha, South African foreign minister in the last dog days of apartheid, was also booked on but ended up taking a different flight. However this theory might seem less credible when you consider that a Swedish diplomat at the United Nations and two US intelligence officers *were* on board.

Around two years after the tragedy the finger of guilt for those responsible stopped pointing at Iran and Syria and instead was gestured in the direction of Libya. In 1991, the USA suddenly needed the support of Iran and Syria in holding together the coalition to take on Iraq in the Gulf War. To include two countries in this coalition that not long before had thought to have been a sponsor of terrorist activity against the United States would have seemed curious. So the prevailing point of view from Washington and compliant countries in the West at least suggested that these two countries were no longer responsible and Libya was. With the conviction of al-Megrahi the case seems to have been concluded concerning culpability. However Jim Swire, the spokesman for the UK Families Flight 103 Group, (his 23-year-old daughter Flora died on board) recently stated that he believed the villains were the ones thought responsible at the time. 'We're convinced beyond reasonable doubt that Iran was behind it and that Syria acted as a mercenary for Iran and that it had little if anything to do with Libya,' he told *The Guardian* newspaper in November 2002. That did not stop the UK and US governments placing sanctions on Libya until they handed over the two suspects for trial.

Certainly the conviction of al-Megrahi looks dubious and the result of the trial – one Libyan guilty, one innocent – looks politically expedient. Al-Megrahi's conviction rests on the evidence of a Maltese shopkeeper that associates the Libyan with placing the bomb on board in a suitcase that started its journey in Malta. Another theory has it that the bomb was placed on board by Syrian operatives, probably at Frankfurt Airport. Whether or not al-Megrahi's appeal turns out to be successful it is likely to prove high profile. He was recently visited in prison by the former South African president Nelson Mandela who is supporting his claim that he is innocent.

No independent inquiry has ever taken place in the UK about how and why Lockerbie happened, despite repeated calls from the families of victims. No one is holding their breath that the government will order such an inquiry. A few people undoubtedly know the truth. But it probably lies in the murky world that is inhabited by governments and secret services. Do not expect any of them to give up the secret too soon.

TOKYO, 20.03.1995: MURDER IN THE SUBWAY

Sarin: 'Organic phosphorous compound used as a nerve gas.'

Many of the prophecies and doomsday scenarios that are ventured by experts warn of chemical attacks on urban populations with the prospect of thousands, maybe millions, being potential victims. It seems a terrifying sci-fi image of the future. But maybe it is not far-fetched and futuristic as it seems – not if relatively recent events in Japan are anything to go by.

On the morning of 20 March, 1995, a religious group that went by the name of Aum Shinrikyo (Supreme Truth) launched a gas attack on the Tokyo Underground. Aum members carried six packages onto underground trains, punctured the packages – made out of nylon and wrapped up in newspapers – with umbrella tips, that released deadly sarin gas into the atmosphere. By the end of the attack 12 people were dead and more than 5,500 people were injured. Many of those injured suffered uncontrollable coughing and vomiting fits. These included medical staff who had been the first to arrive on the scene. Common symptoms of those who were unfortunate enough to breath in the strong smelling sarin included not only vomiting but difficulties in breathing, chest pains, a loss of co-ordination and blacking out. However, this is not as bad as sarin gets: scientists believe that if the chemical mixture had been stronger (the batch used was not, apparently the most deadly form of the nerve gas) the number of fatal casualties would have been enormous and probably running into five figures. The underground is used by up to five million people every day.

The attack was planned for the height of the morning rush hour, around 8am. The plan was to place up to 11 small containers of the gas on trains running on the major lines of the Tokyo underground as they converged at one of the system's busiest stations, Kasumigaseki. This station also happens to be the major stop for many of those working in government. It is close to various ministry buildings including the Japanese equivalent of the Treasury and the Foreign Office. It is also close to the central headquarters for the Tokyo Police. At first it was thought that the attack was a carefully planned assault upon the institutions of power and those who ran them in Japanese society. Subsequently, it turns out that although it was definitely well planned the attack was not quite as conspiratorial in deed as at first thought. It seems that the Aum Shinrikyo leadership thought they were to be arrested at any moment (for crimes already committed, see below) and had lashed out in pre-emptive fashion.

The organization for the attack was thorough. Those who carried out the attack were divided into teams and given specific assignments to leave sarin parcels on particular lines of the underground. One Aum member left his deadly parcel on the busy Chiyoda line. A team of two placed sarin on the Hibiya line and a further duo placed some on the Marunouchi line. Others were selected as lookouts and getaway drivers and all reported to one individual who oversaw the attack. After carrying out their attacks the various teams returned to a hideout where they were given their own injected antidote to sarin. They also burned the clothes they were wearing during the attacks as well as the umbrellas used to pierce the packages (a curiously old-fashioned way of committing such an attack that in all other ways was hugely futuristic). The group tended to attract intellectuals and the sarin was home-made by Aum members.

This highly organized attack reflected the fact that it was not the first attempt by Aum to hit the Tokyo Underground. On July 4, 1995, the group had left four parcels containing sulphuric acid and sodium cyanide in rest rooms on the Underground as well as one in a mainline railway station. No one was hurt as the devices failed to discharge any of their chemical cargo. Just two months earlier, on May 5, 1995, five members of the cult had placed bags of cyanide in a men's toilet on the Underground. Tragedy was averted when a passenger noticed the suspicious looking parcels. In the same month the group also struck when it posted a letter bomb to Yukio Aoshima, the Tokyo Governor. The parcel exploded in the hands of his secretary blowing off the fingers of his left hand. A year before – in June 1994 – Aum members sprayed sarin gas from a car in a residential neighborhood district of the central Japanese city of Matsumoto. The apparent targets this time were the three judges of a district court presiding over a case involving Aum. Residents had filed an action against the cult. Seven people were killed and 270 injured in this attack, including the judges. In previous years, Aum was also responsible for the murder of four people for which a senior member of the organization, Kazuaki Okazaki, received the death sentence.

The leader of Aum, 47-year-old Shoko Asahara (whose real name is Chizuo Matsumoto) is still on trial (the Japanese legal system is famously slow) for ordering the March 1995 attacks on the Underground. Seven people have already been sentenced to death for the part they played but lawyers for Asahara claim that disciples of the sect had misinterpreted his teachings and that he never preached murder. Asahara founded Aum in 1986. The sect's aim is to 'teach the truth about the creation and ultimate destruction of the universe'. In the late 1980s it contested elections without success and the group became increasingly more controversial amid accusations that it brainwashed its members. The group, around 1,100 strong, increasingly came to believe that Armageddon was inevitable and prepared for this 'eventuality'.

It drew on Buddhist, Hindu and yoga teachings and its main deity was Shiva, the god of destruction. It believed the world was heading for a catastrophic end and only those who could protect themselves could help give birth to a new society. The real question of why it carried out the attacks has never been fully answered. The sect continues to operate but has changed its name to Aleph and has sought to distance itself from its recent past. On the fifth anniversary of the attacks the new cult leader Tatsuko Muraoka apologized for the deaths on the Underground and said the group, believed to be funded through computer companies that it runs, would offer compensation to victims. Embarrassingly for the authorities, it was discovered that some of these companies had provided software for Japanese police and defence agencies. In July 2001, Russian authorities arrested a group of Russian Aum followers who planned to set off bombs near the Imperial Palace in Tokyo as part of an operation to free Asahara from jail and then smuggle him to Russia.

LUXOR, 17.11.1997: BLOODBATH AT THE TEMPLE

'It is beyond understanding,'

Hans Wiesner, a tour rep for some of the victims.

On 17 November, 1997, 62 people were murdered at the 3,500 year-old Temple of Hatshepsut, Luxor, one of the greatest archaeological attractions of Egypt. The dead were 58 foreign tourists and four Egyptians. The victims were from several countries. Worst affected was Switzerland. Thirty-five of the dead came from Switzerland and another victim lived there. Nine Japanese citizens were killed, including four couples on their honeymoon. Other victims included three Britons, including a baby and its mother, four Germans, a Bulgarian, a Colombian and a further victim from France. As well as the large loss of life, the attack was shocking for the savagery of those who carried it out. The tourists were gunned down and knifed. Those who tried to escape were hunted down and then viciously slain in a gun battle lasting two hours as the terrorists fought with the Egyptian police. Six of the terrorists responsible for the attack were killed. Two policemen died also. More than 80 people were injured.

Claiming responsibility for the attack was the group known as Al-Gamaa al-Islamiyya (the Islamic Group), a militant fundamentalist organization. The group said its motivation was to secure the release of its spiritual leader, Sheik Omar Abdul Rahman. Rahman is serving a life sentence for organizing the 1993 bombing of the World Trade Center in New York. It denied that it had wanted to kill any of the Westerners at Luxor that day and said that those responsible for the deaths of the tourists were junior members of the organization who did not understand that they were not meant to murder. The attack though followed a pattern of assaults launched upon Western tourists in Egypt. In the preceding five years 34 foreigners had been killed. At the same time the armed struggle between Islamic terrorists and Egyptian police had left around 1,100 Egyptians dead. Almost four years after the attack an Egyptian man took four German tourists hostage, also at Luxor, but this was linked more to a domestic dispute with his German wife rather than an attack on the West.

Despite the November 1997 attack being admitted by Gamaa al-Islamiyya, many fingers have pointed at Osama bin Laden as being behind the murders. Both the Swiss and Egyptian authorities have claimed that bin Laden was behind the financing of the massacre. How much of this is truth, and how much is political expediency on the part of both countries is still unclear. The Swiss have stated publicly that they believe that bin Laden's cash was used. This ended a claim for compensation it was pursuing from the Egyptian government and helped restore bilateral relations between the two countries again. For the Egyptians, anxious to rescue one of its biggest industries – the 1997 attack is reckoned to have cost Egypt billions of pounds in lost tourist revenues – blaming bin Laden was also useful. It proved to the West that Egypt is a country safe for them to visit and not a state under siege from fundamentalists.

The attack in Luxor was not the first by Al-Gamaa. It had been responsible for assassinating the former Speaker of the Egyptian Parliament. A three-decade struggle was launched in the 1980s by Islamic fundamentalists opposed to the pro-Western line taken by the Egyptian government first in signing a peace agreement with Israel, and then by aligning with the West in its 1991 invasion of Iraq. At the same time as the attacks by Islamic supporters, the Egyptian government arrested thousands of Islamic adherents, holding anywhere up to 30,000 political prisoners. Dozens have also been executed.

In 2002, five years after the attack, Al-Gamaa al-Islamiyya claimed that its violent struggle was over, declaring – perhaps somewhat belatedly – that fighting with the Egyptian government was no longer in the interests of the country's Muslims, or Islam generally. Its sister organization, Egyptian Islamic Jihad, had also been responsible for the murder of the former President Anwar Sadat in October 1981. One of the organization's leaders, Safwat Abdel Ghani, also denounced the September 11 attacks in the US in 2001. 'The fighting which took place [in

Egypt] split the nation, damaged the interests of society, and brought no advantage to the people. Therefore, it becomes meaningless, and prohibited under Islam, because it did not lead to guiding people to God's path, but rather caused a greater degeneration,' said Ghani in the summer of 2002. The Egyptian government, at a time of increased international tension, was only too pleased to highlight the fact to the West, and especially Washington, that it no longer had its own 'Islamic problem' and just as important that there was no links between groups there and the al-Qaeda network.

Following the restoration of relations between the Swiss and Egyptian governments, compensation amounting to more than £2 million for the victims' families was agreed by travel and insurance companies. As a footnote, in the summer of 2002, the Brazilian authorities announced that it arrested Mohammed Ali al-Mahdi Ibrahim Soliman close to his home near the city of Sao Paulo, for his part in the Luxor attack.

DAR-ES-SALAAM/ NAIROBI, 07.08.1998: US EMBASSIES BOMBED

On 7 August, 1998, 252 people were killed and 5,000 people were injured when the US Embassies in Kenya and Tanzania were bombed. Over 200 of those killed were Kenyans. Only 12 were American. The attacks were committed in both countries' capitals, Nairobi and Dar-es-Salaam. Kenyans and Tanzanians could not believe they had become terrorist targets, even if the bomb was placed at the American embassy. There was a great sense of injustice within both countries with many feeling that Kenya and Tanzania had been wrongly targeted and punished for the 'sins' of others.

The embassies were soft targets and just months later the

United States government ordered the temporary closure of seven diplomatic missions within Africa amid fears of further attacks. The embassies in South Africa, Kenya, Tanzania, Mauritania, Nigeria, Senegal and Djibouti were all closed. The attacks were immediately blamed, not for the first time, on the terrorist network of Osama bin Laden. Despite this, there were also unsubstantiated claims of responsibility for the bombings by a group known as the Islamic Army for the Liberation of the Holy Places. It claimed to have carried out the bombings in protest at American influence in the region and called for 'the withdrawal of US and western forces from Moslem countries in general and from the Arabian Peninsula in particular.'

However, the belief that the bombings were the work of al-Qaeda continued and in May 2001, four men were all convicted for their part in the atrocities. The four were Khalfan Khamis Mohamed, 27, a Tanzanian, Mohamed Rashid Daoud al Owhali, 23, a Saudi, Wadih el Hage, 40, a Lebanese-born US citizen, accused of conspiracy, but not direct involvement, in the bombings and Mohamed Sadeek Odeh, 35, of Jordan, accused of helping plan the bombing in Kenya. Other defendants, including *eminence grise* Osama bin Laden, remain at large. Prior to the 11 September attacks, this was considered to be bin Laden's worst terrorist outrage. Certainly bin Laden's culpability seems more plausible when considering the text of a communiqué released just after the bombings. This said the embassy bombings were to avenge 'the injustice meted out by the American government to all Muslim nations' and 'the coming days will, God willing, see that America meets a black fate similar to what happened to the Soviet Union. There will be more attacks. More and more Islamic groups will appear that will all fight against American interests.' The announcement was said to have been made by the Islamic Army Organization, which was closely linked to bin Laden.

The American response was swift and hugely controversial. On 20 August, 1998, then-president Bill Clinton ordered US armed forces to carry out retributive strikes on the terror groups thought responsible. 'Terrorist related facilities,' according to the president were bombed in Afghanistan and Sudan 'because of the threat they present to our national security.' One of the sites hit was a pharmaceutical plant in Sudan. This had been identified by US intelligence agents as a precursor chemical weapons facility that had links to bin Laden. The site was used for the preparation of nerve gas claimed Washington. However, serious doubt has been cast on this accusation with many critics claiming that instead of striking back at the terrorist organizations the US had instead merely bombed a pharmaceuticals company in its anxiousness to deliver retribution and, almost as important, to be seen to be striking back. The American strike was seen as a break in policy by many as previously under Clinton, the US had relied mostly on sanctions when dealing with groups it did not like. Sudan had been on Washington's list of states that sponsored terrorism for the five years previous to the August 1998 bombings. Striking back with the military was not the only weapon though. Assets owned by the Islamic Army Organization were also frozen.

If the effect was to try and quell anti-American feeling in the region it was a sadly misguided policy. Anti-American demonstrations erupted throughout the Islamic world in response to the attacks. In Pakistan, demonstrators burned an effigy of President Clinton and called for the destruction of the United States. Security warnings hinted that the American embassy in Germany was under threat of an attack but this threat never materialized. Relations between the Kenyan government and public and Washington also soured, with many in Africa feeling that the American government was only interested in the casualties of its fellow countrymen and women. There was also the concern that there was not enough international aid to help a poor country recover from such a blow. One of the enduring images of the bombings was the rescue work being done by hand rather than any machinery. Comparisons were made between the amount of money offered in compensation and the billions of dollars spent increasing security at embassies around the globe. Compensation offered ranged from about $500 for light injuries to around $11,000 for the loss of life.

OMAGH, 15.08.1998: A NEW LOW IS REACHED

On 15 August, 1998, the single worst ever terrorist atrocity in the history of Northern Ireland was committed. A car bomb placed in the heart of the small County Tyrone town of Omagh killed 29 people and injured over 220. The bomb was designed to cause maximum damage. It was planted to explode on a Saturday afternoon – at 3pm – when many people were in Omagh shopping. It was also the day of the town's carnival. It was a 500lb bomb. A false warning had been given that took many shoppers into the path of the blast. The telephone warning had suggested that the bomb was in a car next to Omagh's courthouse. Instead, it was located almost 500 yards away, outside a crowded shopping mall, and exploded as security forces ushered shoppers away from the court.

Among those killed was an 18-month-old baby and a pregnant woman as well as Spanish students on an exchange trip. Many of those who survived suffered horrific injuries. Many of the most severely injured were among those who had heeded warnings to wait behind protective police lines after the false warning was given. 'Bodies were torn to pieces. I saw a two-year-old child with smoke coming out of its body. There was a man on the street and his leg was lying beside him,' said one eyewitness. 'People were running and screaming everywhere. There was pandemonium. I have never seen so much blood,' said another.

The bombing came at (another) crucial time in the Northern Ireland peace process. The Good Friday Agreement, which paved the way for political devolution and was signed by all major parties within Northern Ireland, was thought to be the main political target. Within days of the attack, Sinn Fein's president, Gerry Adams, said that the 30-year war mounted by republican terrorists had ended. At the same time the British Prime Minister Tony Blair told parliament the Omagh bomb had failed to break the Good Friday consensus for a peaceful future in Ireland. It is clear though that the bomb continues to cast a shadow over the tortuous process to try and establish a long term peace and political settlement in Northern Ireland.

Responsibility for the bombing immediately focused on the dissident terrorist group, the Real IRA, a breakaway group from the Irish Republican Army who had rejected the direction of the peace process with the London government and the move away from violence taken by the IRA. However the process to bring anybody to justice for the attack has been troublesome – and controversial – at the very least. During the original investigation nearly 80 suspects were questioned, over 2,000 people were interviewed and more than 3,000 statements were taken but only one person was charged. The police detained 12 people immediately after the attack but they were subsequently released. Within months of the attack a police officer leading the investigation broke down while begging for help from the Republican community to help track down the terrorists responsible. In February 1999 there was a breakthrough when a builder and publican, Colm Murphy, was charged with conspiracy to cause an explosion likely to endanger life or cause injury.

Facing stinging public criticism for the apparent lack of headway being made in the police investigation, in September 2000 the police set up a new team of detectives in a fresh push to bring the perpetrators to justice. In October 2000, BBC television broadcast the name of four men who it claimed were responsible for the bombing of Omagh; just over a week later Irish police arrested three men in connection with the bombing. Two days later they were released without charge. By March 2001, the victims' families had launched a £2 million fund to begin a civil fight against the Real IRA. The families issued a civil writ which named those responsible for the terrorist attack as Seamus McKenna, Michael McKevitt, Liam Campbell, Colm Murphy, and Seamus Daly.

Within weeks the police were accused of knowing about the attack days before it happened but failing to act upon intelligence that had been gathered. This was an accusation vehemently denied. However in December 2001, a report into the inquiry found that police had received warnings but these were ignored, key suspects were never questioned and the investigation into the murders was strewn with errors. Astonishingly, the Chief Constable of the Northern Ireland Police Service, Sir Ronnie Flanagan, responded by saying he would resign and commit suicide in public if the accusations of failures were true. He later produced a report which claimed that allegations of wrongdoing by the police were 'factual inaccuracies and unwarranted assumptions.' But in February 2002, he was forced to resign as the Northern Ireland's chief constable.

In January 2002, the first conviction in the case was achieved when a Dublin court found Colm Murphy guilty of conspiracy to cause the Omagh bombing. He was jailed for 14 years. At the time of going to print the peace process in Northern Ireland has stalled with the suspension of the Northern Irish parliament amid claims of a spying scandal at the heart of power in Belfast.

ADEN, 12.10.2000: ATTACK ON THE USS *COLE*

Prior to the 11 September attack the previous terror assault on the USA was the suicide bombing of the USS *Cole* warship in October 2000 which killed 17 sailors and injured a further 37. The attack happened as the $1 billion warship, a destroyer, was refueling at the port of Aden in Yemen. Two men on a small dinghy – packed with 225 kilogrammes of high explosives – pulled up to the *Cole* and rammed their craft into the ship. As they did so they stood to attention. The plan was, it was widely considered, to sink the *Cole*. Although the attack failed to achieve this intention, a 13-metre hole was blown into the ship's hull, serving to signal Washington how vulnerable its troops were in the region. The tactics seemed mightily crude but highly effective.

The *Cole* was heading to the Gulf as part of the US Fifth Fleet and was monitoring the compliance of the Iraqi government with United Nations sanctions when the attack occurred. It was the first US warship to be attacked since 1987. The Americans had been patrolling the Gulf since August 1990, the year a UN embargo was established prohibiting the selling of Iraqi oil except under the supervision of the UN as part of that organization's oil-for-food plan.

The tactics were repeated in June 2002 as a suspected plot by terrorists was uncovered, so it was reported, to ram a dinghy into a NATO warship, possibly US or British, in the Straits of Gibraltar. Moroccan and Western intelligence apparently thwarted the attack though. Those thought responsible for both the deaths on the *Cole* and the thwarted attempt in 2002 were terrorism's old friend Osama bin Laden and the al-Qaeda network. Ever since the *Cole* was attacked, Washington has been convinced that al-Qaeda was the group that sponsored the terror assault. Several suspects have been arrested as the Yemeni authorities clamped down, and just as importantly, were seen to be clamping down, on terrorism so as to maintain its fragile relationship with the US.

In November 2002 a major coup was trumpeted by the authorities in hunting down those considered responsible for the attack. Saudi-born Abd Al-Rahim Al-Nashiri was arrested. He was said to be one of the masterminds behind the attack, and was also allegedly involved in the 1998 US embassy bombings in Tanzania and Kenya (see above). He is also thought to be a committed follower of bin Laden's and one of the highest ranking officials of that organization caught since the 11 September attack on the United States. Interestingly, it seems he was also a member of the Mujahadeen, the American backed/created Islamic army in Afghanistan, which has, in many respects, metamorphosed into the al-Qaeda network. The USS *Cole* was taken back to port in the United States, patched up and is now ready to rejoin the 'War on Terror'.

NEW YORK, 11.09.2002: THE WORLD TRADE CENTER ATTACK

Whether or not the attack on the US on 11 September 2001 was indeed the worst in terrorist history – that really depends on your own definition of terrorism – it is clear that it is the single most important and recognizable act of terrorism ever. Its impact can be demonstrated on several levels. First, there was the enormous loss of life that currently stands at 3,038. This includes not only those within the World Trade Center but also those on the planes and in the Pentagon. It also includes the 18 hijackers.

The victims came from more than 90 countries, a figure unmatched by any other terrorist attack. Also the actual way the attack was carried out was pretty well unimaginable to most everybody on the planet – certainly many of those among the American secret services. Then there is the fact that the terror was being carried out on American soil. Here was the world's most powerful regime being humbled and bloodied by an army financed by a man who lives most of his time in a cave. The fact that it was basically carried out in front of the world's television cameras – showing and replaying the shocking and deadly images from New York – adds to the impact. And indirectly, the numbers killed should not be limited to those just on the East Coast of the USA on that day. They led to the convening of the international coalition of the 'War on Terror', the subsequent downfall of the Taliban regime in Afghanistan, and the probable thousands killed there in bringing that regime to its knees, as well as the possible assault on Iraq.

It has left the USA in a position of international dominance unparalleled in the modern world though how easy it is to exercise that power is questionable. September 11 has also left the world in a state of political flux with its people from Australia to the Americas in a heightened state of fear. The actual economic impact is also vast and it is likely that hundreds of billions of dollars have been lost since 11 September across many industries.

The actual events of that day have, somewhat predictably, also spawned a host of conspiracy theories. These include the fact that the attack was somehow carried out by Israeli secret services, that the Americans were aware of the attack about to happen but realized any attack on its home soil would give it a pretext to follow a more hawkish foreign policy across the globe. Theories still circulate that there were also explosive devices placed within the WTC, hence the reason the Twin Towers appeared to collapse so easily. Another focuses on whether or not Flight 93 (the plane that crashed neither in New York or Washington but in a remote spot in Pennsylvania) was actually brought down by an American F-16 fighter *after* the hijacked passengers had reclaimed control of the plane. Other factors are, if not conspiratorial, unclear. These concern whether other planes were almost hijacked that day and what support the hijackers received from staff working at various airports. Why did the President wait so long to react on the morning of 11 September? (He was reading stories to schoolchildren at the time of the attacks on New York) And why did the authorities round-up so many suspects immediately after the attacks if they had no knowledge of what was going on beforehand?

Whatever the conspiracy theories claim there are some basic facts about the day's events. Four planes, hijacked by terrorists using little more than airline cutlery, were either flown or crashed into four separate sites in the USA. At 8.46am on 11 September, American Airlines Flight 11, travelling from Boston (Logan Airport) to Los Angeles crashed into the North Tower of the World Trade Center killing all 92 people on board. Apparently, most people at the time thought this was a tragic accident rather than a terrorist attack. At 9.03am a second plane – United Airlines Flight 175 also flying from Boston to Los Angeles – crashed into the South Tower of the WTC. Sixty-five people on board died. This was too much of a coincidence and confirmed that what was unfolding was a massive terror attack. By 9.21 the US authorities had halted all flights at American airports, the first time that had ever happened in history.

At 9.38am, American Airlines Flight 77, flying from Washington (Dulles Airport) to Los Angeles was deliberately crashed into the Pentagon killing 64 people on board. Seven minutes later the White House was evacuated. At 10.05am, the South Tower of the WTC collapsed. Five minutes after that a portion of the Pentagon collapsed. At the same time, United Airlines Flight 93, travelling from Newark Airport in New York to San Francisco crashed with 44 people on board south east of Pittsburgh in rural Pennsylvania. At 10.28am the North Tower of the WTC collapsed. Seventeen minutes later all government buildings were closed. At 4.10pm building seven of the WTC also collapsed. A little over 2,800 people were killed at the WTC and a further 125 died at the Pentagon. A further 44 people perished on Flight 93.

Responsibility for the attacks has constantly been laid at the door of Osama bin Laden and his al-Qaeda terrorist network though never conclusively proven. There does seem little doubt though that the organization and planning to carry out the hijacking of the planes required a group sophisticated, meticulous and well enough funded to carry out such a large operation. That alone points to an experienced terror group like al-Qaeda. A hunt for bin Laden was launched almost immediately after the attack. This has so far proved unsuccessful despite American forces apparently being close to catching him in early 2002 in the Tora Bora mountains in Afghanistan. But his whereabouts remain unknown (educated guesses place him in the remote areas of Pakistan) or even whether he is still alive. A tape released in November 2002 seemed to prove the fact that he is still alive as the voice, verified as bin Laden's, spoke about the attacks on Bali carried out in October 2002.

BALI, 12.10.2002: THE NIGHTCLUB BOMBING

After the attacks on 11 September, 2001 and the West's declaration of the 'War on Terror' the world waited to see where and when the next attack would be. That there would be an attack was almost inevitable. Despite continuing small scale terrorist attacks, on 12 October, 2002, on the Indonesian island of Bali the world got its answer.

Almost 200 people, mostly Australian tourists, were killed in a bombing outrage at a popular tourist resort. Two bomb explosions took place in two bars at Kuta Beach. One was in the Paddy's Bar and the second was in the Sari Club late on a Saturday evening when the bars were almost packed to capacity with tourists. The explosions took place within six seconds of each other. As well as those who died, around 200, another 132 people were injured. The first bomb was triggered by a mobile phone while the second and much larger bomb was in a minibus parked outside the Sari Club. Those killed or injured in the blasts came from at least 20 different countries. As well as the high number of Australians, 33 British tourists were killed, three Danes, two Americans and at least nine Indonesians. Other countries with casualties included Canada, Ecuador, France, Germany, Japan, South Africa, South Korea, Taiwan and New Zealand.

The attack was seen in many quarters as a direct attack on Australia and its government's unflinching support for Washington's 'War on Terror' (Subsequently, Canberra has announced its readiness to supply Australian troops in any eventual invasion of Iraq). Up to 20,000 Australians were on the island at the time of the bombing. An al-Qaeda suspect subsequently arrested by Indonesian police said the attack was actually aimed at the USA. More broadly the attack can be seen as one visited upon the West in objection to its continued actions in the Middle East. 'I see this very much as a piece of the anti-Western character of these extremist terrorist groups,' said Australian Prime Minister John Howard after the attacks. The site chosen for the bombings was hugely symbolic. Although Bali is a predominantly Hindu island, Indonesia is a mostly Muslim country, and Kuta Beach was enormously popular with Western tourists, especially Australians. It could also be seen as a punishment of Indonesia, for 'giving away' East Timor, the newly independent country that used to form a subjugated part of Indonesia. Alternatively, Australia had belatedly supported independence for East Timor, at the time of the Indonesian invasion in 1975 and it was fair to say Canberra was not too troubled by Jakarta's imperialist act.

The responsibility for the attacks has been blamed on Jemaah Islamiah (JI), (Islamic Group). In November 2002, Indonesian police (who were initially attacked in the West for their attempts to find those responsible but have moved much more successfully than their Western counterparts after the attacks on 11 September) arrested the 'mastermind' behind the Bali bombs. Imam Samudra, a 35-year-old Muslim leader, was picked up on the north-western tip of Java while apparently trying to travel to Sumatra. Samudra, a native of Java, has allegedly frequently visited Afghanistan and learned to make bombs there. He subsequently 'confessed' to the crime. Up to 10 people were thought to have been involved in the team that planted the bombs.

The attacks also seemed to confirm the increased presence of al-Qaeda in South East Asia. JI is a group thought to have close ties with al-Qaeda. There had been warnings for some time that this is the area where the next terrorist outrages would be executed. It appears that these grizzly prophecies have been borne out once again calling into the question the efficacy of the relationship between different governments and their secret services. The CIA (which, admittedly does not have the finest record when it comes to this sort of thing) issued an intelligence report listing Bali as possible target for terrorists just a fortnight before the attacks. The USA subsequently changed its travel notice twice after 20 September in response to threats identified by the CIA, urging Americans and Westerners to 'avoid large gathering areas known to cater primarily to Western clientele including certain bars, restaurants and tourist areas.'

John Howard, on 15 October, 2002, was forced to concede – after initially dismissing the same reports – that the Australian government had indeed received the intelligence that identified Bali as a possible target, but had decided not to change its advice to Australian holidaymakers travelling to Bali. The British government was also forced to issue a clarification concerning what it did and did not know regarding the threat to Westerners in Bali. New advice for travellers was, however, issued by governments after 12 October. The Bali bombings look sure to have further political fallout. The Indonesian government is under intense pressure to prove to the West that it is a serious supporter of the 'War on Terror'. South East Asia is likely to prove an important area in the war. The bombing has reinforced the position of the Howard government, despite internal criticism from many Australians that that was precisely what caused the attack in the first place. The murky world of intelligence, how good it is, how much governments take notice of what is told them by their security services is also under the microscope again.

5 STATE TERRORISM

*'Please forgive us, we don't know what was done in our name.
Please forgive us, I don't know how you could.'*

Natalie Merchant provides a more realistic appraisal of the
murdering and torturing of the Nicaraguan Contras than
Ronald Reagan's description of them as 'Freedom Fighters'.

*'In the battle between good [however defined] and evil [however
defined] it is always the people who get killed.'*

Eduardo Galeano

STATE TERRORISM is difficult to define in the first place. If we think about our primary concern here with the deaths of innocent people it becomes more so. Again we have the problem that often terrorism as an explicit tactic is in some ways a function of weakness; something which will be engaged in on a hit and run basis. So it is likely that this is something that powerful states will accuse weaker ones of. Thus we could easily have a situation where more powerful states may be more effective in evading the label 'terrorist' but may also be directly responsible for the deaths of many innocent people. We should also say that saying that a state is 'a terrorist' is simply a pejorative label; we need to be more precise. Are we saying that the state harbours terrorists or that it funds terrorists? Or are we saying that it uses, funds or encourages the use of methods of terrorism internationally in order to promote its own agenda, or else to keep its own people living in a state of terror domestically?

There are thus many reasons why a state might be labelled as terrorist, and why it might deny it. Israel, a state founded as we have seen on the terrorism of Irgun, and the Stern Gang now characterizes similar Palestinian atrocities as terrorism. Meanwhile its own policies, which keep Palestinians living in terror and apartheid style repression and kill significant numbers of them too, are known as 'counter-terrorism' and are even justified as part of some noble Western crusade (for that is, alas, what it has almost become) against terror. The academic arguments for defining state terrorism could expand almost infinitely. However, if a state is responsible for – or actively funds or otherwise supports those responsible for – the deaths of innocent people the effect is terrorism, whether or not it is given that name. This is clearly a topic then which cannot be done justice in a chapter of this length in a book which is primarily seeking to understand the minds of, and describe the actions of, the types of group more traditionally described as terrorist. However, in the section on further reading are many references which back up, illustrate or embellish many of the points which can, of necessity, only be sketched here. As previously, there is material here which will not be absorbed comfortably, even by the most open minds, but careful further investigation will, we believe, corroborate the existence of a much more confused and morally gray world than might be suspected.

Because of the caveats inserted above, what is attempted here to look at cases where innocent civilians have been killed. Since 1965 several thousand people have been tragically and pointlessly killed by non-state groups from suicide bombings in the Israel, to Enniskillen, to Lockerbie, the World Trade Center and Bali. Meanwhile around 2.5 million have been tragically and pointlessly killed by state actors. So this is not an academic attempt to dissect the unsubtle differences between terrorism and counter-terrorism, between a 'state of terror' and a 'terrorist state', between 'terrorism' and 'terror tactics'. Instead, we refocus on why and when innocent people are killed by the actions – direct or indirect – of the state. The conclusions are not clear cut but they are worrying nonetheless.

The United States – and with no little justification – regards itself as the target of a serious global terrorist threat. It also suggests that particular states are either behind this threat or harbouring those who might carry out such attacks. The United States is ready to condemn such 'rogue states' and even to attack them as part of a 'war on terrorism' which some argue will not end in our lifetimes. Indeed this whole book suggests that if it continues to be fought as it is, it is much less likely to end in our lifetimes. But whether in short or longer-term perspective we cannot doubt that citizens of Western nations, and perhaps particularly the United States as leader of the Western world, face a level of danger from terrorism today which exceeds previous similar threats, for instance from left wing radicals in the 1970s.

Cindy Combs notes that 'nations such as Libya, Syria and Iran have repeatedly been accused of involvement in state-sponsored terrorism' (1997, p.7). There is no sense in denying the unsavoury nature of many such regimes. Whilst this chapter recognizes the existence of evidence against these states, it also asks why, in fact, the United States has *also* repeatedly been accused of state-terror. What have been the bases of such claims against a country which declares itself world leader and bastion of the free world? Why have intelligent commentators labelled the US itself the 'rogue state' and a hyper power out of control? Is there any basis in this claim or do we just dismiss those who are not unquestioningly with us as automatically against us?

The important question about accusing the USA of terrorism is: 'why *would* anyone say that?' Clearly politics plays a part in all judgements about the propriety of state behaviour and so it would be foolish to suggest that negative claims about the United States are in any sense neutral. However, we came to this book not only with the aim of describing – as we did in the previous chapter – the various groups in the world dedicated to killing innocent people to advance their own agenda, but also to looking at the issue of how and why innocent people die unnecessarily. Here there is a wealth of historical evidence which tends to indict the United States. Regardless of such historical evidence, we must also ask whether we really can right the World Trade Center wrong by killing even more people in Afghanistan, in Iraq and beyond? We doubt it and suggest it is simply likely to widen the circle of killing.

The United States has claimed on many occasions since the Second World War to be doing good by taking actions which have resulted in many deaths and total devastation. Vietnam is the best-known example. And so, of course, if we define terrorism as the death of innocents the United States could thus be easily, in this sense, branded as terrorist or supportive of terrorism. And it is worth noting again that even patriotic Americans have described its foreign policy as 'arrogant and cruel' over the period (Hertsgaard, 2002). The United States' more critical historians note that the USA has been the most warlike nation on earth. After the Second World War the USA was already in Korea within five years and then funding the French in Indo-China, before actually taking on the job and bombing not only Vietnam but also Cambodia and Laos in the 1960s and 70s. In the 1950s the US helped covertly remove governments in Iran and Guatemala and in the 1960s sent troops into the Dominican Republic and huge amounts of aid to Indonesia, which were used (with US knowledge) to kill hundreds of thousands in an internal war and also, starting in 1975, to brutally subdue the population of East Timor. In the 1980s Central America's bloodbath was encouraged by US funding in El Salvador, Guatemala and Nicaragua in particular. Though condemned by human rights groups and even the World Court it described its efforts as being in the service of freedom and democracy. (Zinn, 2002). The USA is the only nation to be formally found guilty of terrorism through its mining of Nicaraguan harbours. This catalogue of violence is by no means exhaustive and can be added to by mentioning Chile, Panama, Grenada, Iraq, Afghanistan, Sudan and Yugoslavia. It does not include US funding for repression in Turkey, Israel, Colombia, Argentina and so on.

Of course the very obvious counter argument is that in many – or even all – of the cases alluded to the USA was acting out of the best intentions and on the side of good against evil. Rather than offer this justification others might still justify it by arguing that the USA had no choice; it was, after all, embroiled in a Cold War, and has latterly become the world's policeman. These conflicts were not for the faint-hearted; battles had to be fought and heads banged together. In other words that the USA was doing good by doing bad. These arguments are not ignored, but we should ask ourselves at the outset about who has the right to kill innocent people; if not terrorists then why the USA?

Given limited space and to try and make use of these points more effectively, this chapter is accompanied by a number of country studies. In each case further investigation will be illuminating we are sure. Some of these case-studies are those states which the USA has 'repeatedly accused' of terrorism. Some are countries in which others have also 'repeatedly accused' the US government of terrorism. The reason for this is not unreasoned US-bashing but because we believe this offers important lessons for how the USA – as the world's first hyperpower – should lead the battle against terrorism into the new century. Its power could undoubtedly be an ally in this 'war', but, we ask, does the historical record not suggest the need to match wisdom, compassion and a commitment to multilateralism to that power? It also needs recognition that this is a war of ideas.

THE UNITED STATES IN THE COLD WAR: DID THE END JUSTIFY THE MEANS?

Of the many insults that might be levelled at Jeanne Kirkpatrick, in an odd sense 'hypocrisy' could not be one of them. Ignorance, lack of understanding and compassion perhaps, but not hypocrisy. She was influential in the Reagan administration and came to his attention and prominence in 1979 when she produced an article justifying United States support for authoritarian regimes, presumably including the attendant torture and loss of life. Such justification was based on the idea that authoritarian regimes formed a bulwark against Communism and were therefore the lesser of two evils. She also suggested that such regimes were more amenable to positive change than their totalitarian left-wing equivalents. This sleight of hand allowed continued and increased support for some of the world's most barbarous regimes, especially in Latin America, and included the training of crack troops in methods of so-called 'counter-insurgency' at the US' military/CIA 'School of the Americas'; methods which undoubtedly included torture.

Should we call, though, the consequent deaths of innocents, via US training and support, terrorism or support of terrorism? Brian Jenkins writing within the environment of the RAND Corporation – not known for anti-Americanism – makes the crucial point here that the use of the word 'terrorism' implies a moral judgment. Moral judgments are much easier to have accepted by those with power and 'if one party can successfully attach the label terrorist to its opponent then it has indirectly persuaded others to adopt its moral viewpoint.' (1980, p.65). The corollary is, of course, that it is very difficult to get the label 'terrorist' to stick to an actor already possessing of great power. It is for this reason that Jenkins suggests that terrorism be defined by the nature of the act, not the cause. If we define terrorism by the act, the USA – as some of our country studies offer evidence for – ought at least to be regarded as implicated in terror to a degree which we hope would worry the majority of its citizens.

In fairness, Jenkins is not the only authority on this question. Hoffman disagrees with him; he thinks that Jenkins' view is unsatisfactory because it fails to 'differentiate clearly between violence perpetrated by states and by non-state entities such as terrorists.' (1998, p.33). But we find Hoffman's argument to be the unsatisfactory one; where civilians are targeted should not both be condemned? Should we really exclude Stalinist atrocities, or those of Hitler, because they have been perpetrated in the name of the state? We think not. By focusing on 'acts' rather than 'actors' we believe 'terrorism' acquires a more consistent meaning, even if it is one which can obfuscate academic arguments. The examples below clearly illustrate this point that the state can and should be regarded as terrorist.

CASE STUDY: **STALINIST USSR**

'*The revolution is incapable either of regretting or burying its dead.*'

Josef Stalin

'*The guilt of Stalin and his immediate entourage before the party and the people for the mass repressions and lawlessness they committed is enormous and unforgivable.*'

Mikhail Gorbachev, 1987

Stalin's inclusion in the world hall of infamy is well documented and well earned. Any man who is attributed with the phrase that 'one death is a tragedy, one million is a statistic,' and means it sounds as if he has been touched by evil. Stalin was a despicable man, ruthless leader and ultimately murderous tyrant but to see his story as merely the rise of evil is one-dimensional. He was responsible for sending millions of people to their death, of creating one of the world's most paranoid states, arguably even sowing the seeds of the USSR's ultimate downfall. He also transformed an agrarian society into the second most powerful nation on earth. He was an expert murderer and consummate politician.

Born, Joseph Vissarionovich Djugashvili in December 1879 in the Georgian town of Gori, Stalin was the fourth child of a cobbler: the previous three had died in infancy. As a youth he became committed to left wing causes and spent time in jail in his early 20s for being a socialist agitator. He sided with the Bolshevik party in their struggle for reform of Tsarist Russia, soon progressing his way up the party's hierarchy. During the October 1917 Revolution his role was muted. His main role in the first years of the USSR was pushing through constitutional reform. Lenin, in the months up to his death in January 1924, grew to deeply mistrust Stalin (the nickname means 'man of steel') and advocated that he lose his job within the Bolshevik hierarchy.

However, after Lenin's death a power struggle ensued through which Stalin was able to position himself as leader of the Communist Party and ultimately the country largely because others never treated him as a serious rival. It was a gross miscalculation. One by one he removed rivals and their supporters from the Politburo and by 1929 the cult of the personality surrounding Stalin was already being cultivated.

This 'cult' enabled him to launch his first major agrarian reform, which was to have dire consequences for millions. Blaming poor agricultural output on wealthy smallholders (kulaks) he collectivized farming and sent millions to their death through a policy of brutal repression of the kulak class.

His approach to industrialization was similarly brutal with the nationalization of the major industries, where the human cost was also extreme. There was a method behind the madness (though that is no excuse). Stalin told business leaders his plans were designed to ensure that the USSR survived. 'We are fifty to a hundred years behind the advanced countries. We must make good this lag in ten years. Either we do it or they crush us.'

Political reform was equally tough. In November 1932 Stalin's wife Nadezhda killed herself. This seemed to act as a spur to the 'Great Leader' (his own title) to rid the political classes of his opponents. Perhaps this was the one death that was the tragedy that spurred him towards policies that treated millions of deaths as a statistic. The first sign of the Great Purges to come occurred in 1934 with the assassination, at Stalin's orders, of Sergei Kirov, leading to the repression of millions through expulsions in the Bolshevik Party and reprisals against 'opponents' throughout the country. By the end of 1938 he had murdered, through show trials, most of the old Bolshevik leadership that had come to power at the same time as him. In 1940, the one-time darling of the party, Leon Trotsky, was murdered with an ice-pick at his home in exile in Mexico.

By exterminating the old class Stalin was free to call on the loyalty of the new political intakes and use the state as an ever-increasing weapon of repression and mass terror. Throughout this time he used the state to portray him as a wise and benevolent leader, kindly and intelligent. The sheer brutality of his regime, particularly in the years of the Great Terror (1936–38) is unimaginable. From his political rivals he moved systematically through society; show trials sent police, industrial, cultural and military elites to their death. After these he moved onto the next strata in the pecking order. He used the general population to spy on each other. Different nationalities were also brutalized in order to stamp out possible opposition to his tactics outside Moscow. His policies became increasingly anti-Semitic. The true number he sent to their deaths probably totaled somewhere around 20 million.

The best way to capture or understand anything of the terror of the times nowadays is perhaps through literature. Novelist Alexander Solzhenitsyn recounts the story of a plumber who received eight years' hard labour for turning down the loudspeaker in his room when the daily broadcast of Stalin's speeches came on the radio. His neighbour denounced him. Solzhenitsyn's *One Day In The Life of Ivan Denisovitch* and *The Gulag Archipelago* both describe the appalling conditions in the labour camps of the time, mostly based in Siberia. Anatoli Rybakov's *Fear* is a superb account of the lives lived by ordinary Soviets under the regime of Stalin, and Arthur Koestler's *Darkness At Noon* gives an insight into the sort of loyalty demanded from those with status within the Party. Perplexing, horrific and laughable at the same time, these and other works of literature explain Stalinism better than a hundred history books ever could.

The Red Army's defeat of the Nazis in the Second World War (during which another 20 million Soviet lives were lost compared to 300,000 Americans) and 'Uncle Joe's' determination to remain in Moscow during the war cemented his popularity. Despite his murderous attacks he was genuinely popular with many. How? He massively transformed the lives of millions used to the squalour and degradation of the former Tsarist regime. He made the USSR a modern country, throwing open education and health services to those previously excluded from such basics. He made an intensely proud country the world's second nuclear power and defeated hated historical enemies such as Germany and Poland at the same time. Stalin died at the age of 73 on 6 March 1953 after suffering a stroke and brain haemorrhage. Terror followed him into death. Legend has it that no doctor wanted to pronounce him dead for fear of reprisals. And just in case he was not...

CASE STUDY: **NAZI GERMANY**

The story is too well known to be described in all but the briefest terms here. Possibly because Hitler was an enemy as opposed to Stalin who was an ally, the sordid history is better known than the story of the Gulag Archipelago written about so passionately by Alexander Solzhenitsyn. But despite its horror, it is a story which bears recalling if only so we can bear in mind the need for tolerance as well as vigilance against misuse of power. Hitler's terror state worked because of its sheer ruthlessness; to speak out was to associate yourselves with Jews, or Communists or homosexuals and, of course, to invite your own execution. As with Stalin, and others, you were either for or against: there was no middle course open. That will always be a dangerous message in a free society.

CASE STUDY: **POL POT'S CAMBODIA**

The Khmer Rouge began a large-scale insurgency against Cambodian government forces in 1970, quickly gaining control over more than two thirds of the country and growing rapidly. The United States' role in provoking or stimulating this action is rarely addressed (Chomsky, 1985) but in any case, by 1975, and led by Pol Pot the Khmer Rouge had set up Democratic Kampuchea and carried out radical social reform intended to return the country to 'Year Zero'. For this to happen, cities were evacuated, schools and factories were closed and the population was forced into collective farms. Here intellectuals and skilled workers were assassinated in what became known as the Killing Fields. The radical transformation of society also meant that many others starved as production collapsed.

CASE STUDY: **IDI AMIN'S UGANDA**

Idi Amin was a former British colonial army sergeant and heavyweight boxer, who seized power in a coup in 1971. During his eight years in power in Uganda, he is said to have been responsible for the deaths of up to half a million people. Many more were imprisoned and tortured. Among the thousands butchered in the state research bureau was a cabinet minister, an Archbishop and hundreds of army officers. On seizing power, he rounded up members of the military who had failed to support his coup and executed them. Those who remained ransacked the country in brutal fashion. It is reported that people were found with genitals, noses, livers, and eyes missing and prisoners were forced to bludgeon each other to death with sledgehammers. In 1972 Amin announced that God had visited him in a dream and told him to expel Uganda's Indian and Pakistani populations, who owned almost all of Uganda's businesses. A once thriving nation, Uganda became a wasteland hit with disease, high inflation and a government $250 million in debt after Amin's terror. Idi Amin now lives in luxury in Saudi Arabia.

So it is quite clear, we believe, that violence committed against the people of one country, either by its own government alone or supported by an external actor, very definitely qualifies as terrorism of a sort. In theory, therefore, we can therefore accuse any state of terrorism and should judge it against its record in terms of the deaths of innocents. In a world where 'might' appears to be 'right' terrorism is a difficult label to pin on some states, but the evidence ought to be examined.

CASE STUDY: **VIETNAM**

Vietnam was the original threat of a good example. On independence from France, Vietnamese leaders sought genuine national development and largely ignored the interests of foreign investors. They did not seek aid from the USSR or China and quoted the US Declaration of Independence in their documentation in a clear attempt to elicit US help. Alas the US chose instead to define the Vietnamese as communists and in 1965 the US invaded south Vietnam with its troops believing they were repelling a Communist invasion from the North. But, as John Pilger reports, for one of those troops, Robert Muller, who was decorated for bravery, 'It didn't take long to have that explode into the myth that it was. Vietnam was a lie. It was a lie from the beginning, throughout the war, and even today as they are trying to write it into the history books.' Despite the lie, and the skewed Hollywood depictions, the United States proceeded to decimate Vietnam and its population in a war in which the greatest tonnage of bombs in history was dropped, in which more than one million Vietnamese were killed and a bountiful land devastated. And at the war's final end, despite agreeing to pay substantial sums to help with reconstruction, the US instead left a war-ravaged Vietnam to fend for itself. As punishment for their audacity in defeating the United States, they became the victims of a twenty-five year Western embargo.

CASE STUDY: NICARAGUA

Nicaragua has a long history of domination by the United States which included a US citizen, William Walker being its President in the 1850s and the US government controlling border taxes and maintaining the rights to construct a trans-Isthmian canal through Nicaragua, ultimately, in fact, built in Panama. By the 1920s the US sought to maintain control painlessly by helping train a local national guard to keep the country safe for its interests. This national guard ended up directly at the service of one family who ruled Nicaragua ruthlessly and continuously for the 50 years up to 1979. In that year a popular revolution ousted the dictator Anastasio Somoza and brought to power a government committed to social reform, boosting literacy and raising the role of women in Nicaraguan society.

What the new Nicaragua regime actually did, however, seemed to matter little as the United States saw only the threat of communism. Others have more accurately described the revolution's radical social reforms as the threat of a good example. (Melrose) Whatever view one takes of the situation, the United

States helped form, fund and arm a terrorist organization to fight a war against Nicaragua who became known as the Contras. Although this group committed unspeakable, deliberate atrocities well documented by Amnesty, Human Rights Watch and church groups for instance, US President Ronald Reagan chose to call these particular terrorists, freedom fighters. When Congress decided that the Contra rebels' terrorism should no longer be funded, groups of 'patriots' decided to give Los Angeles the gift of crack to help continued (and illegal) funding via the illegal sales of arms to Iran.

In the case of Nicaragua the United States is accused not only of the state sponsorship of terrorism, but is actually a convicted terrorist. In 1986 the World Court found the United States guilty of launching attacks on Nicaraguan territory, of laying mines in Nicaraguan territorial waters and of supplying the Contras with a CIA manual which encouraged acts contrary to humanitarian law. At its 'School of the Americas' the United States has trained militaries from all over Latin America in such acts and is so responsible for the deaths of many innocent people not only in Nicaragua but also in Chile, Argentina, Colombia, Guatemala and El Salvador to name but a few. The reaction, by the way, to the judgment of the World Court in 1986 condemning the US for 'unlawful use of force' against Nicaragua was simply to denounce and ignore it. When the General Assembly of the United Nations then passed a resolution calling on all states to respect international law, the USA voted against it joined only by Israel and El Salvador.

CASE STUDY: EL SALVADOR AND GUATEMALA

The situation in Nicaragua encouraged the United States to continue funding and providing advice to the regimes in El

Salvador and Guatemala, both guilty of incredible barbarity and gross human rights abuses. This was justified in the Cold War climate by arguments, like those of Jeanne Kirkpatrick, that it was better to support authoritarian governments than risk social reform – a living wage, union rights and paid holidays being just a step or two from communism, obviously. In both cases the United States found the activities of military official and unofficial death squads somewhat inconvenient in terms of ensuring continued funding. In El Salvador a state department white paper called 'Drawing the Line in El Salvador' sought to prove Cuban and Soviet links to guerrilla forces in order to continue funding. The authors later admitted they had lied. In any case, such help that did arrive can in no way have justified widespread torture and terror.

In Guatemala, the activities of the 'counter-insurgency' G2 forces was so horrific that funding actually stopped, although, conveniently, the shortfall seems to have been made good by the US partner in barbarity, Israel. Despite occasional doubts the United States remained steadfastly committed to militaries who were steadfastly committed to massacring their own populations. Aryeh Neier of Americas Watch and Helsinki Watch (human rights organizations) suggested that 'gross abuses of human rights are not incidental to the way the armed forces of El Salvador conduct their war against the guerrillas. In our view, the principal reason that those abuses continue at such a high rate at a point when – one would guess – the armed forces should have run out of politically suspect persons to murder is that the murders instill terror. Terror is the means whereby the armed forces maintain their authority.' (Chomsky, 1985, p.26). This is an armed forces heavily funded by the USA and the comments are particularly true of elite, US-trained battalions such as Atlcatl.

CASE STUDY: **CHILE**

11 September is also the date of the CIA-backed coup in Chile which brought General Pinochet to power. His regime dropped dissidents from helicopters, kidnapped and tortured over 3000 people in a 17-year reign of terror. General Augusto Pinochet Ugarte was, seemingly yet one more military dictator from the dog days of South American politics, the 1970s – just another leader in the production line of brutal rulers in charge during that period: a man who took power from a democratically elected government by the use of force, who ruled his country with an iron fist and whose regime chased and murdered opponents at home and overseas. In his time in power it has been predicted that over 16,000 people were exiled imprisoned, tortured and assassinated.

The exact number will never be known. Thousands more Chileans 'disappeared'. Torture was a deliberate and well-used instrument of the Pinochet state. His forces even carried out a political assassination *in Washington* in September 1976 when Orlando Letelier a foreign minister in the Salvadore Allende government, the one Pinochet seized power from, was killed by a car bomb.

So far so predictable. However, the General has come to be remembered long after his military counterparts who ruled at the same time in say Uruguay or Argentina has been forgotten. Pinochet has come to represent a deeply important position in the history of state terrorism and all those leaders that commit terror during their tenure in office. His 1999 arrest by the British authorities on the request of a Spanish judge, Baltasar Garzon, for crimes against humanity during Pinochet's 16-year tenure in office sent a clear message to those who commit state terror that they are answerable for their actions when in office. Although subsequently released after a complex legal process in 2000 his detainment had ramifications not only for Pinochet, whose legacy has now been almost completely destroyed, but for other leaders, present and former, who feel their actions may lead to their arrest.

The General's political career and subsequent infamy came well into his military life. Indeed it seemed that his lack of political ambition was the reason he found himself in such a high position in Chilean society in the first place.

Born in 1915 in the port of Valparaiso it was his mother who pushed the young Pinochet into a military career. The military in Chile had a long-established tradition of Prussian discipline and loyalty and, unusually for South America, political independence. Pinochet rose through the Army's officer corps and cut his political teeth by heading a government clampdown on the Chilean Communist Party.

By the 1960s and early 1970s, Pinochet had risen to the top of the military tree and was about to launch upon the actions that would make his name known around the world.

In 1970, after a number of near misses at the polls, Chile voted in the first democratically elected Marxist president in the Western Hemisphere, Salvadore Allende, who embarked upon a series of far-reaching socialist reforms including the nationalization of foreign-owned assets in the mining, communication and banking industries. This radical programme, along with land reform, polarized the nation.

Deeply unpopular with the middle class in Chile, Allende had also stirred the wrath of foreign interests and governments, specifically the US. Washington, through the CIA helped organise a growing opposition to Allende and the massive campaign of political subversion and social unrest culminated in a military coup on 11 September 1973.

Right up to the moment of the coup, many in the Popular Unity government of Allende dismissed fears of a military takeover because of the Chilean Army's record in staying out of politics.

Just three months before the coup, Allende had promoted Pinochet to commander-in-chief of the armed forces because the General was thought to be a man who could be trusted.

Allende was very wrong and Pinochet was thrust centre stage.

Salvador Allende died on 11 September, as Pinochet's troops took control of the country, in circumstances never entirely clear and Pinochet hel control for the next 16 years.

From the earliest days of his rule Pinochet was quick to suppress those who showed any hint of opposition. As well as the thousands who were rounded up, tortured and killed in football stadiums, used by the authorities as mass detention centres, political parties were banned and trades unions were suspended. Anybody known to be on the left of the political spectrum was a target. Pinochet has a habit of lambasting critics for being "Marxists' which borders on the almost pathological.

His rule was largely brutal – in 1974 the secret police which carried out many of Pinochet's orders in suppressing political opponents, the Direccion Nacional de Inteligencia, was formed – and was sometimes comical in retrospect: soldiers were allowed, for example, to cut the hair, in public, of young men whose locks were deemed to be too long.

Although he at first did not seem to have a penchant for politics by 1974 he had appointed himself president defending his actions, as he often did, as those of a patriot whose actions had halted Chile from a slide into chaos and, more specifically (though in Pinochet's case it means the same thing), communism. This was the time of the Cold War after all, and this ensured that his government received support from the outside world.

The US, happy that its interests in the country had been restored, deflected criticism of Pinochet's human rights record by showing the advances it had made economically.

The 'Chilean miracle' where a ravaged, second-world country overturned its economic fortunes through a slavish adherence to free-market philosophies was hailed by Western leaders of the time such as Ronald Reagan and Margaret Thatcher. Pinochet's policies, based on those espoused by academics at the Chicago School of Economics were marked by market deregulation and privatisation – the very policies being pursued in Washington and London. This made Pinochet very popular in the West, even more so given the hatred of communists shared by Reagan and Thatcher. In political parlance, Pinochet was 'one of us'; his human rights record could be ignored because of his adoption of pro-Western economic strategies and, by his hatred of communism, he was firmly in the West's camp.

The economic miracle though has been discredited of late: over the whole period of Pinochet's rule, the Chilean economy fell 6.4%, was one of the poorer performing economies in the region and per capita gross domestic product was lower in 1993 than it was in 1973.

All the time the political repression continued.

By the 1980s with his position cemented Pinochet called a referendum on effectively, whether or not his rule should continue – and was decisively rejected by the electorate.

By 1990 he had given up power and civilians once again took over the reins of power but his position in Chilean society remained pre-eminent.

Pinochet was still commander-in-chief of the army and he had packed the courts with judges and statutes that made sure he would not be held culpable for the human rights crimes of his government.It was not until 1998 that he finally gave up his post as commander-in-chief.

In his 80s he continued to enjoy a privileged existence and often travelled to the UK for health reasons and because of his close friendship with Mrs Thatcher.

It was on one of these trips that the General was arrested and began a chain of events that would eventually expose his record to the rest of the world. Although he was finally returned to Chile a free man, the once strong, always proud military man returned to his home in a wheelchair.

It was hugely symbolic.

The strongman of Chile returned to his country a frail, old and broken pensioner with his record of torture and political repression exposed for the whole world to see.

CASE STUDY: **EAST TIMOR**

Having helped Suharto to power and providing him with the wherewithal to literally exterminate problems of dissidence, the USA tipped Indonesia the 'big wink' allowing it to invade East Timor and embark on a campaign of ruthless genocide in 1975. The United States was motivated by oil supplies and like Britain supplied equipment which maintained the slaughter.

THE UNITED STATES AFTER THE COLD WAR: HAS ANYTHING CHANGED?

The examples above are simply that, and fail to cover the full geographical spread of activity. Doubtless horrific detail has been missed. Clearly however, whatever moral qualms one might have about some of the previous information, an important rationalization could be that faced with the Soviet Union – Ronald Reagan's 'evil empire' – the United States really had little choice but to act in the way it did. Indeed in the sense that the United States ultimately triumphed it can at least be argued that the ends have now justified the means, an argument which its communist opponents, of course, cannot use in justifying their own behaviour during this period. The US therefore enters the contemporary period firmly in possession it seems, and despite some of the information outlined above, of the moral high ground.

However, and despite the rhetoric of multilateralism and a new world order, the United States has failed to exercise its power in a moderate and measured way. Instead it has chosen – even when using cloaks of consultation – to use its status as the world's first hyperpower to act unilaterally and with overwhelming force and loss of life. As in the Cold War the United States claims its actions are in the service of a better world, but in doing so it has fallen in love with its own reflection and assumed that what is good for the United States is good for the world. But the world does not want to be dominated by the USA. The section below details some implications of US efforts to rule the world.

CASE STUDY: **IRAQ**

On 2 August 1990 the Iraqi army invaded its southern neighbor, Kuwait. Four days later the United Nations responded by imposing a complete trade embargo on Iraq. Many thousands died in the accompanying war. In the ten years since Iraq has continued to be the subject of sanctions that affect almost every aspect of life for the average woman, man and child. A 1999 UNICEF report calculated that more than half a million children had died as a direct result of sanctions. On average 200 Iraqi children are dying every day. In September 1998, Denis Halliday head of the UN humanitarian program in Iraq resigned claiming he could no longer administer 'an immoral and illegal' policy. His successor, Hans von Sponeck also later resigned, along with the head of the World Food Program. Meanwhile US and UK politicians insist that the sanctions regime is necessary to contain the threat of Saddam Hussein. When asked on US television whether the death of 500,000 Iraqi children as a result of sanctions was justified Madeleine Albright replied 'I think this is a very hard choice, but the price – we think the price is worth it.' Now, after keeping Saddam in power because they didn't want Kurds or Shia Muslims causing trouble in Iraq, the USA has decided to wage war on these people – again – and has made it quite clear that world opinion is irrelevant.

At the time of writing the United States has not yet found the 'courage' to ignore the United Nations and wishes of the majority world wide and to once again act unilaterally to kill thousands more people.

CASE STUDY: **PANAMA**

Manuel Noriega took effective control of Panama in 1983. The US government knew he had been involved in drug trafficking since at least 1972 but he proved useful to the CIA, helping, via drug operations, the US war against Nicaragua. However by the late 1980s Noriega had started to provoke opposition from business leaders, dragged his feet over further help for the Contras and needed to be replaced, since in the year 2000 the Panama Canal would revert to Panamanian control. Economic sanctions by the US hit the poor hard and a coup failed, so in December 1989 the US invaded Panama killing hundreds or perhaps thousands of civilians restoring power to a rich white elite just in time to ensure a compliant government for the administrative changeover of the Canal on 1 January, 1990.

John Pilger – admittedly a noted critic of the abuse of US power – asks how many people must die, routinely, as the global bully stalks the playground. The pretence that high-level aerial bombing does not deliberately kill innocent civilians may be part of US sophistry but this argument is not accepted on the ground. You cannot drop large amounts of explosives from a great height and then say that civilian deaths are an accident; well actually you can say this, but that does not make it right. The US willingness to act unilaterally, to decide on what issues and how it will act without regard to international sentiment, and above all its willingness to kill innocent civilians (or see them killed by its weaponry) has built a level of international resentment from which the US will find it hard to recover. The war against terrorism is being lost before it starts; a more constructive, genuinely humanitarian and fair (for instance over Israel) foreign policy could be a much more effective weapon than the current policy which is akin to chopping off one head always to see two grow in its place.

It is worth noting here that 'understanding cannot diminish the horror of the atrocity committed against the innocent' (Hopple and Steiner, 1984). But at the same time some level of understanding, beyond simply 'we American, you evil' might be useful. As already quoted in our introduction, noted American statesman George Kennan, writing on rising terror in nineteenth century Russia notes that if you wrong a man 'deny him all redress, exile him if he complains, gag him if he cries out, strike him in the face if he struggles [then] at the last he will stab and throw bombs.' (In Combs, 1997, p.29). At the global level the

United States must look at itself from without and ask whether terrorists (individuals or states) are simply evil or if there are constraints of global politics which encourage them to lash out in unreasonable fashion. Since this is only a question we should not be afraid to investigate; look not at the rhetoric but at the facts of various international events and it is difficult not to say to George W that 'you go about things the wrong way'.

CASE STUDY: COLOMBIA

US state terror is clearly present. Here the rightwing paramilitary United Self Defence Forces of Colombia (AUC) (responsible for the bulk of massacres, assassinations and threats that have forced more than two million rural Colombians to flee their homes since the late 1980s) is a crucial part of the US Plan Colombia, the allegedly anti-guerrilla, anti-narcotics military drive funded by the US to the tune of over $1 billion. Despite official US denials the AUC declares that Plan Colombia would be almost impossible without its paramilitary forces who report daily to the military. A 1996 report by Human Rights Watch described Colombia's military-paramilitary partnership as 'a sophisticated mechanism, in part supported by years of advice, training, weaponry and official silence by the United States, that allows the Colombian military to fight a dirty war and Colombian officialdom to deny it.' AUC paramilitary groups routinely assassinate unionists, *campesino* leaders, human rights activists, judges, progressive politicians and journalists; attack residents of resource-rich or strategic rural areas; and slaughter and displace entire communities of unarmed civilians. In the late 1980s and early 1990s, paramilitaries obliterated the leftwing Patriotic Union Party, systematically assassinating thousands of its candidates and members. Yet US military aid to Colombia has ballooned from an average of $60

million a year between 1992 and 1995 to around ten times that
amount requested by President George W. Bush in 2002 and all of
that on top of the $1.3 billion for Plan Colombia that President Bill
Clinton signed in 2000.

CASE STUDY: **KOSOVO**

The disintegration of Yugoslavia after 1991 did not have the
same impact on the United States as the Iraqi invasion of
Kuwait. Vital US interests were not threatened and so ethnic
cleansing was not opposed, somewhat giving the lie to US
claims of being at the service of, and acting for the salvation of,
humanity. However US public opinion and the credibility of
NATO did require some action and the US-sponsored Dayton
peace accords sought to resolve the situation in 1995. Although
progress was made, the book was effectively closed on Serbian
leader Slobodan Milosevic's crimes, who then turned his attention to the province of Kosovo where the majority Kosovar
Albanians had become increasingly unhappy with centralized
rule from Belgrade. Serbian intimidation of the Kosovar population was finally met with a US-led NATO bombing campaign (of
1999) against Serb targets inside Kosovo and against Belgrade
itself. Nicholas Guyatt poses the question 'was this a rare but
admirable instance of the US backing the right side?' Having
encouraged the situation by its attitude towards Milosevic the
US then used high altitude bombing as the means of punishment when they finally decided to publicize his crimes. This
killed many innocent civilians in Serbia, despite the usual American claim that they were not targeted, and also saw Serbian
troops step up and complete the persecution and expulsion of
the Albanian Kosovars. After the US bombing campaign,
returning Albanians were understandably less committed to

living with Serb neighbours who had, in turn, to flee. The US handed the intractable problem over to the UN.

CASE STUDY: **SOMALIA**

In the aftermath of the 11 September attacks, it is alleged that the ending to the film Black Hawk Down was changed to make it more palatable for US audiences; less critical of US policy. With or without a changed ending the film needs serious questioning. 'The collapse of government in Somalia in 1991 had unleashed fierce fighting between various groups of Somalis, and the resulting instability had brought the country to the brink of mass starvation' (Guyatt, 2000, p.75). A huge US-UN operation did indeed avert the starvation but the US showed no inclination to disarm the warring factions despite warnings from UN Secretary General Boutros Ghali that this would be absolutely essential. Even after most US troops withdrew, the bulk of forces left were US and operational control was in US hands. But the US became fixated on General Aideed to the extent that what had started as a humanitarian operation turned into a situation regarded by most Somalis as an invasion and led to the US packing up and going home after 18 US marines were killed. Estimates of Somalis saved from starvation but then killed by combat start in the thousands.

CASE STUDY: **RWANDA**

Scarred by the experience of Somalia the US then did everything in its power to scale down action in Rwanda in 1994 in order to limit costs. In doing so it was able to set aside its commitments to stop genocide. As the US delayed and then further delayed action by charging for the hire of armoured vehicles even though it is massively in debt to the UN, 500,000 people were shot or hacked to death. 'Reluctant to give up its central role in world affairs but unwilling to commit troops and money for UN operations, the US atrophied the cause of peacekeeping just as the situation in Rwanda required a flexible and dynamic response.' (Guyatt, 2000, p.80).

CASE STUDY: ISRAEL AND PALESTINE

In the earlier history of terrorism some historical background was given to the situation, confirming that the Israeli state – using religious justifications – had used terrorism to ensure the formation of the Israeli state. Since then it has used unswerving and extensive US support to ensure an iron grip over the whole of Palestine including the occupied territories where it has established numerous illegal settlements and connecting roads. Though such settlements are illegal under international law and have been condemned by the UN they effectively make the establishment of an autonomous Palestinian state impossible despite the clear historical and moral claims for such an entity. Clearly, the Jewish population of Israel have historical reasons to fear for their security, but can such security really be bought by the oppression of and insecurity for, others? As John Pilger reports, when the Israeli army attacked Ramallah and other towns in 2002, it was reported as being an anti-terrorist operation. But it was a psychological and cultural, as well as brutal physical, attack on the Palestinian people and the knee-jerk accusations of anti-Semitism which accompany such claims should not discourage people (and it includes some brave Israelis) from denouncing such behaviour. The Culture Ministry had been systematically destroyed in Ramallah, and lest that be felt an accident, Israeli soldiers had smeared their own excrement on the walls, on office equipment and had vandalized an exhibition of paintings made by Palestinian children. This kind of thing, according to Israel is not terrorism – funded by the US – but counter-terrorism. The effects of the occupation are not only felt during attacks such as those in Ramallah. Palestinians also have to contend with day-to-day restrictions on freedom of move-ment. Ordinary lives are a maze of controls, road blocks, checkpoints reminiscent of apartheid South Africa and engen-dering the same angry feelings of frustration and resentment. Israeli has claimed that this is necessary for their security although if that were true it does not seem to be working; it also ought not to be necessary to point out that a suicide bomber, like all suicides, must have become desperate to commit such an act, although the security of Palestinians does not seem a subject for discussion. Suicide bombs are presented to the Israeli public as an insane act by an insane people but a wider analysis would say there is a way out of the suicide bombs. Condemning suicide bombers, and rightly so, is easy, but providing the circumstances in which these people would find avenues of hope instead of avenues of despair, that is the challenge. But instead, in effect Israel is creating its own problem; and as the problem gets worse it makes it worse by transforming Palestinian communi-ties into a prison, surrounded by tanks, walls and fences. Israeli Professor Ilan Pappe argues that 'the Holocaust memory does not allow any moral criticism of anything that Israel does... If you do criticize Israel, you are immediately charged with anti-Semitism.' We must not believe that two wrongs make a right.

It may, of course, seem odd to the casual reader or analyst of politics to suddenly come across the claim that the United States is a terrorist. But though there are moral and other dividing lines between US behaviour and that of Hitler, Stalin or those impli-cated in such terrorist outrages as the Lockerbie bombing it is no mistake. Citizens of the United States should not fling this book to floor in outrage (the argument here is not a personal attack). Uncomfortable though it is, the United States has in many senses reaped what it has sown.

Furthermore, as the acknowledged single Superpower or Hyperpower the United States has insisted on having its own way, turning only to the UN for justification and ignoring it when it pleases, allowing the UN to take on messy clean-up jobs, but not allowing it to function as the world's policeman that it could be. Thus it might seem harsh to criticize the US for inaction, as in Rwanda, or for taking action such as that in Kosovo but in insisting on being in control and by not letting the international community act independently of it, the US has effectively been implicated in the deaths of countless civilians. What is more, its power could have been used for good in more than a rhetorical sense.

CASE STUDY: CUBA

The United States sought to invade Cuba in 1961 and failed. The CIA has since poisoned Cuban crops and made innumerable, if occasionally farcical, attempts on Castro's life. If ever a state was given reason to hate the USA and to become what it has become as a result it is Cuba. In terms of international terrorism however, if Cuba is anti-American it is hardly surprising and if it has had to be tough to survive an unjust US blockade, that seems inevitable too. But US support for Latin American militaries of the most vicious kind mean that there are now many more terrorists living in the United States than those who currently reside in Cuba. For the USA to link Cuba with international terrorism shows up perhaps more than anything else that US arrogance means it is impossible to disagree with the American dream, and anything which challenges it in any way will be regarded as terrorist. This in turn ensures that US state terror will always meet with a terrorist response.

MORE STATE-SPONSORED TERRORISM

Notwithstanding the arguments made above, other states have been involved in activities leading to the loss of life of innocent civilians from other countries. In the cases below we look at some of the claims for regarding various states as state terrorists.

Russia like the United States has a particular and complex history. However, and despite the insecurity and fear which its history has engendered, modern day Russia must, by any universal standard of behaviour, be considered to have been involved in a bloody campaign of state terror against Chechnya. However, in the war against terror, where countries are either for or against 'us', the Russians are an important ally. As with the Colombian military, where an ally in this war against terror is engaging in terrorist practices, we can overlook it. As in Columbia, so it is in Chechnya. Countries such as Iraq, Iran, Syria and Libya have become known as rogue states and implicated in international terrorism. Whilst these accusations are made by the USA, a country with around 200 invasions, bombings and so on to its name in a little over 50 years, we must resist being drawn into the argument that terrorism by Syria, or any of the other 'rogue' states is somehow OK. It is not. At the same time, however, the United States is so determined to control world politics and has so trampled on the sensibilities of others that some kind of lashing out is inevitable. In the current situation where allies in the war against terrorism are often oppressing their own people and where allies like Saudi Arabia are thought to have widespread sympathy for Osama bin Laden (at the level of the man – and it is usually a man – on the street) surely the USA is trying to keep all its troubles locked up in a suitcase which looks nonetheless fit to burst?

6 TERRORISM AND THE FUTURE

INTERPRETING THE PAST, as this book has shown, is one thing. But if looking at history shows us how difficult is analysis of the present, then assessing the future is quite another magnitude of problem. Even so, at the risk of predicting in error, we will now look at the important issue of possible/probable future trends in terrorism, including the issue of whether an end is in sight to the dominant position of this issue in our news programmes and daily lives.

However much faith we have in the resolution of our leaders or in notions such as 'homeland security' and the fact that the public is in a heightened state of vigilance, it is difficult to argue with John Gray (talking in the *New Statesman*) when he argues that 'terrorism must be deterred and subdued, and wherever possible its causes must be alleviated [but] it cannot be eradicated.' (25 February 2002, p.53). Having looked at possible future threats, this is a point to which we return in our conclusion.

The future of terrorism includes not only immediate issues such as 'the Iraq question' and what al-Qaeda might do next but also takes us into the realm of science fiction in terms of the possibility of terrorist methods long thought of as theoretical but now seen as possible and probable; for instance threats such as the uber-modern threat of something called 'cyber-terrorism' and the terrifying possibility of bio-terrorism. Given that events in the real world are likely to overtake 'Iraq' we concentrate here on possible new 'styles' of terror.

Analyzing these possibilities is a task fraught with pitfalls since it is evident that no one can predict the future with any degree of certainty. Those who try invariably end up with at least some egg on their face, although that has not stopped many from attempting such a task before us. Even how you attempt to assess the future is a matter of controversy. The eighteenth century philosopher Edmund Burke told us that: 'You can never plan the future by the past' whereas Abba told us that 'the history book on the shelf is always repeating itself.' With respect to the reputation of Burke his insight seems no greater than that of Sweden's premier pop band of the 1970s. So, although any examination of what is going to happen is hardly going to prove an exact science we can probably suggest that history will probably both help *and* hinder us in arriving at an understanding. However, when all is said and done, we believe that there are certain conclusions we can draw with a certain degree of confidence. It is on the balance of probability and on the basis of arguments made earlier in this book that we seek to advance our claims about the likely future of terrorism.

The first claim about the future is that terrorism is likely to dominate international and domestic political agendas to a degree that has never been witnessed before, straining alliances and friendships as the world seeks to get to grips with a mostly unseen enemy – a kind of international bogeyman – who is constantly emphasized by world leaders to make sure their populations are aware of an ever-present threat. We live in an era of globalization and failed states; neither is new but their conjunction has allowed the terrorist threat to be projected worldwide. While it has reasons and motivations it will be difficult to pin down, much less eliminate, the terrorist threat. But what are those reasons and motivations? We believe – and have stated since the outset – that understanding reasons will be much more important than 'resolve' if terrorism is to be controlled.

But this is easier said than done. Reasons for the bloody slaughter of innocents are always difficult to comprehend, and given the horror we may be disinclined to analyze rationally. Those who engage in this terrorism appear to reject everything, and in a sense they do. The failure to get to grips with the idea of this threat over the last decade, and always to denounce it without attempting to understand it, has been 'part of a much larger inability to grasp the realities of globalization that goes all the way back to Christian Enlightenment faith in history as a teleological process ending in a species-wide civilization.' (Gray, 2002, p.52). What does this mean? In essence that in the Western world many have embraced the dangerous fallacy/fantasy (now violently rejected by terrorism) that Western values can, or should be universalized. As long as 'we' hold on to a belief that ours is the only way, the right way, we can only encourage future desperate rejections; we may find no meaning in such acts but they will continue, not as constructive acts to create a better future (as with some terrorism in the past) but as acts of rejection to the creeping homogenization of global culture. The world has become polarized between those who feel history is laid out before us in the obvious triumph of Western values, and those who reject this but feel they have few powers of expression in doing so. Terrorism has long been the preferred form of expression of the down-trodden from US revolutionaries, through the French Resistance and Nicaraguan revolutionaries amongst many others.

Thus, when George Bush stated to the world that 'you are either with us or against us' he drew a moral line in the sand that every country in the world had to take notice of; but in a sense it was *already* true and is part of the problem. Such a remark could easily be dismissed – world leaders often make remarks on morality – but for the fact he leads a country whose military capability and political power are unparalleled to the extent that it might reasonably be known as the world's first 'hyper-power'. Never before have countries been asked to sign up to such a comprehensive 'struggle' as the one currently taking place against terror. At the time of writing 17 different countries had signed up to supplying troops for the American-led war on terrorism. These include not only the usual suspects such as the UK and Canada but also countries such as the Czech Republic, Finland, Romania and Uzbekistan. And these countries have signed up even though, we are warned, the struggle is likely to be long. 'The war has just begun, there will be many tough fights ahead, but the coalition remains steadfast in its objectives to defeat international terrorism and protect the lives of its people,' read a statement of intent published by the coalition countries in 2002.

And woe betide anybody who questions the moral clarity of Washington, as even countries not normally associated with questioning the US line such as Germany have found out. In the autumn of 2002 the Gerhard Schröder administration failed to subscribe to Washington's thinking on military action against Iraq and found itself derided as 'anti-American' in the US press and was accused of poisoning the relationship between Berlin and Capitol Hill. Its defence was that it was pro-German, these things were said during a national election after all, and that a critical friend is better than a supine one. Viewed from Washington the defence was as strong as Winona Ryder's when it came to denying a charge of shoplifting. This kind of behaviour mirrors what went on a decade ago. In the last Gulf War of 1990 Yemen, a United Nations' Security Council member, voted against US action in Iraq. The US called this vote 'the most expensive "no" vote in history' and cut off aid to Yemen. Syria showed the flexible nature of international politics when in November 2002 it backed US moves for a United Nations' resolution to present Iraq with an ultimatum to accept weapons inspectors into its country or face the threat of war. That is the very same Syria long regarded as a sponsor of state terror. (The move was not well received in Baghdad. On hearing of the news, the Babel newspaper, owned by Saddam Hussein's son Uday, exclaimed 'even you Syria have accepted it! The new resolution is only new in name...it is a confirmation of Bush's aggressive attentions against us.') Intriguingly, the US accuses Syria of having the same motives as Iraq when it comes to obtaining weaponry and even arming Iraq, making Washington's calls for an attack on Baghdad look highly selective at best. 'Syria, through foreign assistance, is seeking to expand its chemical weapons program, which includes a stockpile of nerve agent. We believe that it is developing biological weapons and is able to produce at least small amounts of biological warfare agents. Syria is also pursuing assistance from North Korea and firms in Russia for its missile development programs. The country has become a major transshipment point for goods and technology going to Iraq,' said Under Secretary of State John Bolton in a speech in November 2002. Here it is worth repeating, however, that as long as the US seeks to impose its own vision on the world, it is unlikely to find peace. There are so many contradictions in US policy, even to its own citizens who look closely enough, such as Noam Chomsky, that it will always look faintly ridiculous to the world, as the following parody suggests.

THE CASE FOR REGIME CHANGE

E-mail circular believed to have originated with Ted Rall, author of *To Afghanistan and Back*:

NEW YORK: Making the case for United Nations intervention against the United States, Iranian President Mohammad Khatami told the organization yesterday that military action will be "unavoidable" unless the US agrees to destroy its weapons of mass destruction. In a much-anticipated speech to a special session of the UN General Assembly held in Brussels, Khatami launched a blistering attack against American leader George W. Bush, accusing him of defying UN resolutions and using his country's wealth to line the pockets of wealthy cronies at a time when the people of his country make do without such basic social programs as national health insurance.

'Nearly two years ago, the civilized world watched as this evil and corrupt dictator subverted the world's oldest representative democracy in an illegal coup d'état,' said Khatami. 'Since then the Bush regime has continued America's systematic repression of ethnic and religious minorities and threatened international peace and security throughout the world. Thousands of political opponents and ordinary citizens have been subjected to arbitrary arrest and imprisonment. Basic civil rights have been violated. This rogue state has flouted the international community on legal,

economic and environmental issues. It has even ignored the Geneva Conventions on the treatment of prisoners of war by denying that its illegal invasion of Afghanistan which has had a destabilizing influence throughout Central Asia was a war at all.' Khatami said the US possessed the world's largest arsenal of nuclear weapons, weapons 'that, when first developed, were used immediately to kill half a million innocent civilians just months after acquiring them. No nation that has committed nuclear genocide can be entrusted with weapons of mass destruction. Bush has invaded Afghanistan and is now threatening Iraq. We cannot stand by and do nothing while danger gathers. We can't wait for this tyrant to strike first. We have an obligation to act pre-emptively to protect the world from this evildoer,' Khatami said.

As delegates punctuated his words with bursts of applause, Khatami noted that US intelligence agencies had helped establish and fund the world's most virulent terrorist organizations, including al-Qaeda, and the Taliban regime that harboured them. "The US created the Islamist extremists who attacked its people on 11 September, 2001," he stated, "and Bush's illegitimate junta cynically exploited those attacks to repress political dissidents, make sweetheart deals with politically-connected corporations and revive 19th century-style colonial imperialism." Khatami asked the UN to set a deadline for Bush to step down in favour of president-in-exile Al Gore, the legitimate winner of the 2000 election, the results of which were subverted through widespread voting irregularities and intimidation. "We favour not regime change, but rather restoration and liberation," he said. In addition, Khatami said, the US must dismantle its weapons of mass destruction, guarantee basic human rights to all citi-

*zens and agree to abide by international law or 'face the con-
sequences'. Most observers agree that those 'consequences'
would likely include a prolonged bombing campaign targeting major US cities and military installations, followed by
a ground invasion led by European forces. 'Civilian casualties
would likely be substantial,' said a French military analyst.
'But the American people must be liberated from tyranny.'
Khatami's charges, which were detailed in a dossier prepared
by French President Jacques Chirac, were dismissed by a representative of the American strongman as 'lies, half-truths
and misguided beliefs, motivated by the desire to control a
country with oil, natural gas and other natural resources.'
National Security Minister Condoleezza Rice denied that the
US maintains weapons of mass destruction and invited UN
inspectors to visit Washington to 'see for themselves that our
weapons are designed only to keep the peace, subject of
course to full respect for American sovereignty.' The UN is
expected to reject any conditions for, or restrictions on, arms
inspections. Experts believe that the liberation of the United
States will require a large ground force of European and
other international troops, followed by a massive rebuilding
program costing billions of euros. 'Even before Bush the
American political system was a shambles,' said Prof. Salva-
tore De Luna of the University of Madrid. 'Their single-party
plutocracy will have to be reshaped into true parliamentary-
style democracy. Moreover, the economy will have to be
retooled from its current military dictatorship model – in
which a third of the federal budget goes to arms, and taxes
are paid almost exclusively by the working class – to one in
which basic human needs such as education and poverty are
addressed. Their infrastructure is a mess; they don't even*

have a national passenger train system. Fixing a failed state
of this size will require many years.'

The 'War On Terror' is now over a year old and threatens to be extended at any point, specifically and contentiously in the direction of Iraq. Attacks by terrorist groups continue, most noticeably the bombing in Bali of bars packed with Western, mainly Australian, tourists on October 12, 2002 which resulted in the death of around 200 people. The constant prediction and fear of further terrorist attacks if not ever-present is somewhere close to it. But, as has been noted, terrorism is not one-sided. If we accept the statement of author Joseph Conrad in his novel *The Secret Agent* that 'the terrorist and the policeman both come from the same basket' then those that act as policeman on the world stage continue to play their part in a violent world.

Nations continue to use the cover of the 'war against terror' to commit terrorist acts themselves. Just ask the Chechens about the new commitment of the Russian government to defeating terrorism having seen 100,000 of its civilians killed in the last decade, and the number continuing to rise since 11 September. Political assassinations of individuals are undertaken by coun- tries – witness the murder of five 'al-Qaeda' operatives in Yemen by the US in November 2002. (A compliant Western press covered this story as a fine example of intelligence and military wherewithal combining to help lessen the threat from terrorists. Imagine the outrage if say, five Western military staff travelling in a car were murdered by forces unknown). And human rights abuses continue by states – again under the cover of the war against terrorism. In many countries, the world community seems to condone human rights abuses by regimes on the basis that they hold back an Islamic tide; we somehow doubt that the way to halt the popularity of orthodox Islamic regimes is through poverty and human rights abuses – again a subject to which we return in conclusion.

But the fact is, whether the story of terrorism is one of Western insensitivity or simply of crazed madmen, it is a long story in which the capacity to commit acts of terror by those inclined to do so is increasing. In fact, flick through any daily newspaper and it is hard to escape a story about terrorism. It is a subject that seemingly will remain a constant in our lives. So what can we expect to happen from here in practical terms?

THE THREAT OF FURTHER TERRORIST ATTACKS

The impetus for this book, like many that have appeared in the last year or so on terrorism, was the attacks on the USA on 11 September 2002. To try and make sense of something instinctively tragic, awful and horrifying is perfectly understandable. Even in the time since this book was commissioned there have been a number of further attacks – and attempted attacks – not only the bombing of tourists in Bali. In late 2001 'shoe bomber' Richard Reid was only just halted from his mission to blow up a US-bound passenger jet. On October 6, 2002 a French ship, the Limburg, was bombed in an apparent suicide attack off the coast of Yemen. Two days later a US marine based in Kuwait was gunned down. Little more than a week later six people died in a bombing in a shopping mall in the Philippines city of Zamboanga. All the attacks were, apparently, carried out by al-Qaeda. (At the same time thousands have been killed in the 'liberation' of Afghanistan but this section will deal with the future of state terrorism a little later on). The general threat of terrorism (whether real or imagined) has never been so great for so many people.

At the same time as these attacks have been carried out – heightening tension among the general population – the fear that an attack will take place is never far away. Since 11 September the American government has given out numerous warnings that further terrorist attacks are both inevitable and imminent. 'All of us are vulnerable,' warned the US Deputy Assistant State Secretary, Matthew Daley. In November 2002 the British government – in a muddled announcement – warned that the 'fanatical extremists' of al-Qaeda would strike again through a variety of methods – either 'a so-called dirty bomb or some kind of poison gas; maybe they will try to use boats or trains rather than planes. The bottom line is we cannot be sure. We cannot be sure of when, where or how terrorists will strike. But we can be sure they will,' was its alarming conclusion. Special rapid reaction military and medical teams have been established to help cope with the consequences of a terrorist attack. These include taking measures such as the mass evacuation of major cities, distributing anti-radiation pills to hospitals and training police snipers to pick off suicide bombers.

There are several conclusions which might be drawn from all of these warnings. First, that to cover the backs of the intelligence services (who mystifyingly remain largely uncriticized by politicians despite being hopelessly exposed by 11 September) governments are issuing warnings to show that they are on the ball – determined to prove that never again shall a government be so exposed as the US was in 2001. However, the number of warnings seems to demonstrate a rather 'blanket' approach such that one wonders if this is more of political manouevre; by their constant warnings our leaders increase their credentials as 'benevolent guardians' showing the increased vigilance we (and the loyal but nit-picking opposition) would expect. One wonders if intelligence has improved or if politicians are simply covering their backs?

Second, we might conclude that ministers are talking tough in order to up the perceived threat from 'evildoers' and countries such as, let's say, Iraq, so they can justify their plans for invasion and 'regime change.' Whatever the press do to try and make the linkages, and indeed however much of an evil tyrant Saddam Hussein is, it seems that artificial linkages are being created between al-Qaeda and Iraq and that Saddam may be more dangerous as a cornered rat than as a rat in charge of his own backyard. (But as we noted earlier, forgive us if events have rather passed these comments by!)

Thirdly, it is not unreasonable to conclude that these attacks really are going to happen. Most likely the warnings are a result of a combination of all three of these factors; politics, justification of policy and reality. Indeed this book has argued insistently that a world is being created, and circumstances exist which make further terrorist attacks inevitable; there seems to be a greater threat nowadays of terrorist attacks than there has been over the past few years and we can expect these to continue.

The US State Department – which does not include things it has supported such as massacres of peasants in El Salvador or extermination of communists in Indonesia – suggests that there were 136 'significant' terrorist attacks in the four decades between 1961 and 11 September 2002. However it is important to note the significant rise in such incidents in the latter half of this period. 86% of those attacks classed as significant have occurred since 1982 and the majority of those in the last decade. If we recall that the world was significantly concerned in the 1970s about the significant leftist terrorist threat this increase upon that level of activity is alarming.

Between 1961 and 1982 US State Department figures count just 19 attacks including the Munich Olympic massacre of nine Israeli athletes in 1972, the assassination of exiled Chilean foreign minister Orlando Letelier in September 1976 (exiled because of a coup by the US-backed military regime of Augusto Pinochet), and the hostage crisis from 1979 until 1981 when 66 US embassy staff in Tehran were taken captive.

Between 1983 and 1995 there was a rough average of three significant attacks each year; a noticeable but not extraordinary increase. But since then the number of attacks has increased dramatically. In 1996 the State Department counted 22 incidents including the bombing of the Khobar Towers in June which left 19 US military personnel dead and an explosion on the Paris subway in December which killed four and injured 86. Using these figures, between 1997 and September 2001 the average number of terrorist attacks increased to just over nine per year. It is surely no coincidence that recent years have been those in which, following the fall of the Soviet Union, the end of the Nicaragua Revolution and so on, the US seems totally determined to ensure that the whole world is opened up to its unrestricted access and that any alternative form of society be regarded as strictly against the rules.

Of course the State Department's figures cannot be treated as exhaustive and as illustrated above, the problem of defining terrorism presents us with a fundamental problem before we even think about counting what counts. Even so, other figures are open to us; Business group Berg Associates, in an assessment of risk to the business community from terrorist attacks actually found the number of attacks falling throughout the 1990s, both the number of attacks perceived as 'anti-US' and international terrorist attacks. It also points out that between 1990 and 1997 more people were killed in 'ordinary' murders in Indianapolis than globally due to international terrorist attacks. Between 1990 and 1997 116 Americans were killed in what the study labels terrorist attacks. Terrorist groups, it also concludes, 'are not proliferating at an uncontrollable rate.' But such findings do seem particularly out of step with the majority of studies.

A far more exhaustive list comes from the Center for Defense and International Security Studies (CDISS). (Again these figures cannot be seen as fully comprehensive as its listing of state terrorist attacks is patchy, and therefore, intriguing to say the least. It includes the July 1985 attack by French secret agents on the Greenpeace ship *Rainbow Warrior*, which killed one person. It also lists the 1998 bombing of Afghanistan and Sudan by the United States against 'terrorist sites', the latter of which turned out to be a medical supplies factory. The attacks occurred, perhaps not coincidentally, at the height of the Monica Lewinsky scandal. It also includes the Chechen attacks on Russian targets though not the rape of that nation by Moscow. Its list is, in other words, extremely patchy). However, that caveat aside the CDISS list seems to be the most exhaustive in existence. It concludes that between 1945 and 1998 there occurred 373 terrorist attacks across the globe. A breakdown of the figures is illuminating. Between 1945 and 1949 there were 21 attacks. These include the attack in April 1948 by the Jewish Irgun group on a Palestinian village, which left 254 women and children dead. In the next decade (1950 to 1959) that number actually decreased to 17 attacks including the 11 September slaying of Pakistani Prime Minister Lisquat Ali Khan by an 'Afghan fanatic.' That figure almost doubled in the 1960s to 33. In 1961 the first United States aircraft to be hijacked was taken over by a man called Ortiz who forced the plane to land in Cuba.

He received asylum in the Caribbean but was jailed for 20 years when he returned to Miami in 1975. At the end of the decade Italian anarchists killed 16 in December 1969 when they blew up a bank in Milan. In the more turbulent 1970s 68 incidents were recorded including 'Skyjack Sunday'. Aircraft from three companies – TWA, Swissair and BOAC were hijacked in Jordan by the Popular Front for the Liberation of Palestine. Four hundred hostages were taken and the governments involved, German, Swiss and British, agreed to the release of a number of terrorists. During the 1980s terrorist attacks climbed to 106. The African National Congress, now the ruling party in South Africa caused an estimated $7 million of damage by bombing oil-for-coal plants in June 1980. The 1990s saw the number jump slightly to 125 including a 1993 assassination attempt by the Iraqi intelligence service on George Bush the First.

The CDISS figures point at an average of seven terrorist attacks each year from 1945 to almost the present day. This figure clearly does not reflect the upward trend of attacks in the past few decades however you account for what happened and by whatever criteria you use to judge what is or is not a terrorist attack. In the eight years of the 1990s used, the number of attacks was around 15 every year, almost the same number that occurred throughout the entire 1945–1949 period. Statistics, of course, have a notorious reputation, but studies such as this tend to point to the fact that despite various differences and anomalous years the number of terrorist attacks is, regrettably, increasing.

But are they increasing at a rate in line with the overriding obsession of policy chiefs throughout the Western world with terrorism? Quite simply, no. Terrorist attacks will continue, of course, but the number of people killed by terrorists when compared to killers such as poverty, AIDS, obesity, malnutrition or road deaths are relatively few. Furthermore, the risk of being killed by a terrorist attack has increased only minutely in the past two decades. The actual effects of the war against terror and the accompanying vigilance and patterns of military expenditure are surely more political than anything else?

But of course, one death is too many and the figures collated rely, almost entirely, on studies carried out before 11 September, a definite line in the sand when it comes to terrorism, and the world, one could argue, has been far more unstable since then. What we might regard as more worrying is that the tactics of terrorist groups have notably changed in the past few years. The portable bomb delivered by suicidal 'operatives' is an important change in the tactics of terrorist groups. The potential for damage, death and destruction has increased greatly through the use of such tactics. This is not only true of the attacks on the World Trade Center and the Pentagon but also of attacks carried out by groups such as Hezbollah and Islamic Jihad in the Middle East and the killings at the US embassies in Kenya and Tanzania and the attack on the USS *Cole* in Yemen. That is the most frightening aspect. But the scale of any attack and the seemingly random nature of recent attacks (this is of course untrue if you consider as symbols of wealth such targets as the World Trade Center and the huge number of holidaying Westerners in Bali) only add to the fear. Fears of dirty bombs and terrorists being able to capture the 'ultimate prize' (a nuclear weapon) serve to heighten an already increasing fear of attack. What has changed here is that such terrorism is based almost entirely in 'nothing to lose' rejectionism; we live in a world where too many people have nothing to lose and until changing this becomes a priority of the war against terror, we are likely to see attacks increase in number.

THE WAR ON TERROR

'Our war on terror is well begun, but it is only begun. This campaign may not be finished on our watch – yet it must be and will be waged on our watch.'

George Bush

'Washington's war on terrorism is as doomed to failure as its war on drugs has been.'

William Blum

'We make war that we may live in peace.'

Aristotle

After the USA was attacked on 11 September, only the most foolish or innocent person would not expect Washington to respond with force. The United States is a country used to using its military forces to 'resolve' problems. Its mindset has often been to call in the military. It was hardly going to stand idly by in the face of the 11 September outrages. The USA also happens to be the world's only superpower with an array of weaponry unseen before, unmatched and unique. The question was not if or even when it would respond, but how.

The War on Terror, responding to 11 September got into full swing in October 2001 with the US bombing campaign of Afghanistan that resulted in the collapse of the Taliban regime later. Officially this was known as Operation Enduring Freedom although originally called Operation Infinite Justice and changed – perhaps because it seemed to many as Finite Injustice? After the campaign – which ensured the collapse of the Taliban regime in Afghanistan, as part of which the United States received offers from 136 different countries for military assistance – Enduring Freedom gave way to Operation Anaconda in which troops from six countries helped to seek out remote al-Qaeda hiding places on the ground in Afghanistan. The removal so swiftly of such a supposedly implacable and obdurate enemy as the mullahs of the Taliban was viewed in many quarters in the West as a significant triumph, though many forgot to mention that the bombing of one of the world's poorest countries by the world's richest was hardly ever likely to be a fair contest.

The noises from Washington have consistently been that the war on terror would be fought for an indeterminate – but long – time against a shadowy enemy whose presence lurks around every corner. It would also be fought against those who housed, helped or harboured them in any way. Its impetus, claimed Capitol Hill, was not revenge but a search for justice and for stability; a desire to hunt down terrorists to stop further outrages occurring. These are laudable motives. But how this is all achieved is a matter of contention. Trying to prepare your general population that they should be braced for a long war is hardly a message that many governments really want to convey (though of course that hasn't stopped many in history from doing so).

Bombing mountains and valleys in Afghanistan is one thing, finding a solution to terrorism is quite another. One thing is clear though – any solution cannot be achieved through military means alone. In partial defence of Western coalition countries this is something that they have recognized. Intense diplomatic manoeuvring, international law enforcement and financial regulation on money laundering through the Organization for Economic Co-operation and Development's Financial Action Task Force have all formed part of a multi-pronged response to terror. However there are two massive tests for those advocating the need for a prolonged war. First, how feasible is the aim given that the means used may just multiply the response. Second, and relatedly, how easy will it be to find political solutions when power vacuums are caused through the result of military action?

Many more innocent non-combatants have died as a result of state actions throughout history (including since 11 September) than have ever been killed by terrorist groups. This helps to ensure grievance and makes it certain that the conditions for further terrorism still exist and are aggravated. Violence breeds violence; a lesson that the world's preponderant military power seems unable to accept either domestically or internationally.

Violence breeds violence is surely more useful as an argument in explaining terrorism than one implicitly put forward by many, namely the belief that terrorists are somehow envious of our lifestyles. That somehow because of jealousy of our greater access to computers, DVDs or a new generation of mobile phones a new generation of terrorists have been unleashed. Or to put it far more eloquently as the novelist Gore Vidal did in an article in *The Nation* in 1998: '...the image of America the beauteous on its hill, so envied by all that it is subject to attacks by terrorists who cannot bear so much sheer goodness to triumph in a world....' Although perhaps the fact that this (the American dream) is sold as something we can and should aspire to, even as it is so clearly limited to the few, does have something to do with it.

So much of today's terror, and the reason why it regrettably seems to have a future, is that it simply thrives on the false promises of capitalism. So much is promised but alas so little delivered that hatred and resentment build up. But this is not just for economic reasons, but for the fact that so much political injustice is also clearly evident in the world. Firstly, the need for a solution to the Middle East problem, specifically the

Israeli/Palestinian issue and secondly, nation building after regime change in Afghanistan and, maybe, latterly Iraq. A solution to the Palestinian issue remains unlikely and in some quarters not seen as central to the ultimate goal of defeating terrorism. Since the 11 September attacks the 'problem' has been contained through so-called 'counter-terrorism', not resolved. And that looks like being the policy for some time to come as, despite a well-documented number of different views held by coalition countries on the subject, moves to resolve it remain a side issue at best. Though, in defence of the hawks, the oft-repeated mantra that terrorist leaders such as Osama bin Laden (if he is still alive) would actually put an end to attacks remains untested. A political solution is often viewed as a way of eradicating terror. It would surely lead to the eradication of a number of groups but should we not expect disenchanted groups to remain much in the way they did in the wake of the fragile peace settlement in Northern Ireland? But as in Northern Ireland so in the world – there are short term political solutions and there are long term political solutions which get to core issues of economic equality and having a genuine political voice.

Nation building is also central to the war on terror and if it is not done successfully, many countries will continue to provide a fertile breeding ground for the recruitment of terrorists. In Afghanistan, the huge numbers killed (more than died in the World Trade Center) may already have inspired many an orphaned Afghani 10 year old to take up arms in the future. The West may well feel that its motives have been clearly demonstrated by events after the defeat of the Taliban, namely, that a non-feudal, nascent pluralistic society with respect for human rights is beginning to emerge. By its own calculations, the US had put some $230 million into Afghanistan in 'humanitarian assistance' by February 2002, when the bombing of the country began, and pledged $300 million in assistance for the whole of 2002. Canada had put in $160 million, Germany pledged almost $70 million and the UK some £60 million. However it does not always go according to plan. In November 2002, the American pressure group Human Rights Watch (HRW) reported that 'US-led coalition forces are actively backing a warlord in western Afghanistan with a disastrous human rights record.' The area under control of one Ismail Khan was known for 'widespread abuses, including arbitrary and politically-motivated arrests, intimidation, extortion and torture, as well as serious violations of the rights to free expression and association.' HRW concluded that the 'friend of the international community in western Afghanistan is an enemy of human rights.' The US government stands accused of arming Khan and his supporters. But this didn't stop US Defense Secretary Donald Rumsfeld calling Khan 'an appealing person.' Of course, it is easy to nit-pick. But, and it would be hard to imagine Rumsfeld or his boss, at least publicly, disagreeing with the next statement, as HRW states in its World Watch Report 2002, that: 'Any fight against terrorism is only in part a matter of security. It is also a matter of values. Police, intelligence units, even armies all have a role to play in meeting particular terrorist threats. But terrorism emanates as well from the realm of public morality. Terrorism is less likely when the public embraces the view that civilians should never be targeted – that is, when the public is firmly committed to basic human rights principles.'

However the fight against terrorism so far has centered on police, intelligence units and most specifically armies, but less on nation building through the use of human rights, claims HRW. 'Many of the policies of the major powers, both before and after 11 September, have undermined efforts to build a global culture of human rights. These governments often embraced human rights only in theory while subverting them in practice. Reversing these policies is essential to building the strong human rights culture needed to reject terrorism.' While the West is prepared to support regimes on the basis of their ability to suppress Islamic forces the war on terror is unlikely to be won. A better way would be to demonstrate that Western style democracy and associated capitalism can deliver in terms of material comfort; but while the West is more concerned to exploit than to help this will not be possible.

Aiding abusers in the fight against terrorism is not confined to those in Afghanistan. In an effort to shore up several fronts the Bush administration has, in its haste, given financial aid to frontline states with lamentable human rights records. These include almost $4 million in military aid apiece in 2001 to Armenia and Azerbaijan. Georgia has received $2,510,000 despite its record of abuses and accusations from Moscow that it harbours Chechen terrorists. Indonesia received $400,000 even though it has long stood accused of being a state terrorist, with torture and rape the weapons of some of its security forces. Kazakhstan received around $1.5 million.

Big winners were Pakistan who received some $50 million for its fight against terrorism – many al-Qaeda operatives are thought to be hiding in remote mountain regions. $18 million went to the Philippines. Uzbekistan received $6 million. Does all this really matter? Well, yes it does when a war is supposedly based on superior principles to those of the enemy, when those prosecuting the war constantly emphasize that the reason they have been attacked in the first place is because of their love for freedom. And the reason why they need to win the war is to safeguard those very same freedoms. Such concerns may be pushed away easily by some but if the war on terror is to be judged for what it can achieve in the long run rather than just bring down the Taliban, then there should be more effective measures of what is actually happening. And a very big test for those principles, that the Western coalition says it is defending, is coming up.

NEW FORMS OF TERRORISM AND COUNTER-TERRORIST INTELLIGENCE

If injustice in the world, particularly economic and political, remains a feature which inevitably gives rise to a terrorist backlash and means terrorism will remain a force in future years, we also need to point out that the particular historical juncture makes particular forms of terror more likely. If the rejectionism of religious fundamentalism combined with modern communications makes attacks more likely, it also means that methods will be used which would not be possible if the terrorist wished to survive. You can hide a bomb and depart the scene, but if life is not an issue you can fly or drive much bigger bombs or release poisonous gas and of course take much bigger risks leading to a larger scale of operation.

As well as the scale, and daring (if that is the right word for attacks on innocents) terrorism may also develop (another unfortunate word) in other ways. One word bandied around recently is eco-terrorism; given the unprecedented interest in the environmental state of the planet this is terrorism carried out in the name of the environment, although theoretically we could also apply it to sabotage of the environment rather than efforts to save it. In the section that follows we look at ideas such as eco-terrorism, bio-terrorism and dirty-bombs. We will begin, however, by looking at the intelligence operations needed to combat such threats.

Before moving to these specific types of threat, one of the most pressing areas of battle in the continuing war against terror is within the espionage arena. Whether or not the longer term solutions need to be more subtle than is currently suggested, in the short term the quest for gathering salient and vital information has never been more important.

Ely Karmon in his 1998 book *Intelligence and the Challenge of Terrorism in the 21st Century* says:

To combat the changes in terrorism since the end of the Cold War and into the twenty-first century, national intelligence organizations must increase the use of human intelligence operatives. In the past, national intelligence organizations have placed a heavy emphasis on electronic intelligence gathering techniques. Electronic eavesdropping and satellite pictures provide excellent tools for listening and looking at what terrorists may be attempting. However, there is no substitute for human assessments based on local or regional knowledge. Intelligence agents and analysts must be familiar with the history, language, and customs of many societies. Intelligence agents must be able to understand the particular social, cultural, or historical events that terrorists may be twisting to justify their criminal actions.

All fairly sound stuff but the problem for the coalition security forces is that there seems to be quite a few gaps in their work. One of the first thoughts after the attacks of 11 September was how nobody knew it was about to happen. This turned out to be a misapprehension: some American secret service agents knew that something was about to happen but could not convince their bosses to take their warnings seriously. And these threats were reported to have been communicated to high positions across the American political and defence structures. As we have seen earlier, an appreciation of the political effects of US world domination also led some political analysts to predict what was going to happen with chilling accuracy.

The trouble for the West is that it has been constantly playing catch up when it comes to the intelligence war. Ever since 11 September security has been heightened on plane travel (though not to an extent that gives too much peace of mind) with suggestions that there should be armed guards or even armed pilots to prevent a re-occurrence of what happened. When Richard Reid tried to blow up his shoe there were suggestions, serious ones at that, that all airline passengers would in the future have to travel shoeless. The fingers pointed by the West at the Indonesian security forces in the wake of the Bali bombing seemed a little unfair as well. Reports that an attack in South East Asia was imminent were indeed received but it is a fairly big place. And, again the security forces were then shown to be playing catch up, warning Western tourists to take care when in well-known tourist areas. It is understandable, but to a member of the public, perhaps less than reassuring. In a way it is predictable. When tackling various terrorist groups the governments are for the most part, responding to events. Which makes the need for better intelligence gathering even more important because the ace is usually in the hands of terrorists. They know what events they are planning next and it is the intelligence services' job to try and get that information. So how well are they equipped to do that job? Not brilliantly.

This is especially worrying in the area of South East Asia. Security experts seem to agree that the next area of conflict for the War Against Terror, or more specifically in the fight against al-Qaeda, will be fought in South East Asia. There were predictions of this long before the Bali bomb. After the bombing of

Afghanistan by the US, with a little help from its friends, the loose structure that is al-Qaeda fragmented to various places including remaining in the remoter parts of Afghanistan, Pakistan, Yemen and countries such as Indonesia and Philippines. Al-Qaeda is thought to be recruiting for new members and allies from Pakistan which, given the bombing of the Taliban, continued support for Israel and so on, may not be so difficult. One theory has it that a senior member of the al-Qaeda network is directing the terrorist traffic from a base in Karachi. Support for extremist Muslim causes in many areas of the region is thought to be widespread. American troops have already been sent to fight members of the Abu Sayyaf group in the southern Philippines. However even the presence of troops from such a military power as the US have failed to put an end to the activities of Abu Sayyaf. Singapore and Malaysia also say they have uncovered terrorist cells in their countries.

If the US cannot put a stop to terrorist activities, with all their massive resources, then what hope is there for the regional security forces, with substantially fewer resources to draw on? As one Indonesian officer admitted candidly in the wake of the Bali bomb, 'I have to be honest, our intelligence organizations are in bad shape.' The bombing of Afghanistan after the 11 September attacks has had some effect. The leaders have been killed or at the very least are on the run. There has been significant rupture to its finance network not just because of the bombing but also because of the work of the FATF. Some communications have been obliterated. However, according to intelligence gatherers, the bombing by the US-led forces show what a resilient organization al-Qaeda is. Now, instead of one massive group, the terrorist network has become a much more flexible group composed of various like-minded 'teams' who share an ideology but little else beyond the desire and commitment to continue their armed struggle. The result of all this means that further 11 September-type attacks are unlikely; instead more 'low-scale' but incredibly effective attacks such as the bomb in Bali are likely. Even when they do not happen – such as the alleged plot to release poison gas on the London underground system in November 2002 – they cause alarm and disruption. The fear is that despite its current structure the potential for the group to inflict a massive strike still exists, depending on its ability to get its hands on a 'dirty bomb', a nuclear device or even to target civilian – or military – nuclear plants in the West. The following section considers the nuclear threat, along with the other forms of warfare generally included in the phrase 'Weapons of Mass Destruction'

WEAPONS OF MASS DESTRUCTION

NUCLEAR

The first type of threat most people think of when weapons of mass destruction are mentioned, and by far the most deadly. There are four main aspects to the threat of nuclear terror, which we shall now consider.

Nuclear missiles

The first and most obvious nuclear threat. A nuclear missile fired by a terrorist group at New York, apart from the immediate devastation this would cause, would be likely to start a major war, as the US government would feel obliged to retaliate in kind. However, missile technology, James Bond villains notwithstanding, is beyond the grasp of even most countries, so it is hard to imagine any terror group, however sophisticated, developing an ICBM delivery system in the near future.

'Suitcase' bombs

The technology to build a nuclear bomb, however, as opposed to the missile to deliver one, is alarmingly simple. A recent report by the Nuclear Control Institute (see Appendix A) concludes that a sophisticated terrorist group would find it relatively easy to construct a nuclear device with a payload of around a kilotonne. This would require only 8 kilogrammes of even 'reactor-grade' plutonium, or around 25 kg of enriched uranium. There are unconfirmed reports that al-Qaeda has already attempted to buy material of this nature.

A further concern is that during the 1980s, the Soviet Union manufactured anywhere between 100 and 250 'suitcase' bombs, of which up to 50 may be unaccounted for.

Power plant attack

Requires no knowledge of nuclear technology at all. In this type of attack, the idea would be to cause a meltdown at a power plant, releasing radioactive contaminants into the air. The International Atomic Energy Authority, a firmly pro-nuclear body, has expressed serious doubts about the effectiveness of the security around nuclear power plants, citing in particular the fact that many US nuclear power stations are not designed to deal with an attack from the air. In light of the fact that the 11 September attacks were carried out using hijacked planes, this seems almost unbelievably lax. An attack on a power plant is perhaps the most likely method of nuclear terror; it is potentially devastating, it requires no know-how beyond the ability to hijack a plane, an ability possessed by many terrorist groups, and it is cheap in comparison with building a bomb.

'Dirty' bombs

Not strictly speaking nuclear bombs at all, since their explosive power is not based on a nuclear reaction. A dirty bomb is a conventional explosive device containing radioactive material which will disperse on detonation, causing contamination. Their effectiveness will vary with the nature of the radioactive material, but many experts agree that the main danger from a dirty bomb is from the explosives, rather than radiation. However, the reporting of a bomb which had exploded and spread radiation would inevitably be done in so hysterical a manner as to cause widespread panic; almost terror by proxy.

BIOLOGICAL

Closely linked to chemical terrorism but distinct from it is the idea of bio-terrorism.

Bio-terrorism largely takes the form of introducing disease into areas controlled by the 'enemy' or targeting specific strategic or socially important areas such as crops with various diseases.

Since the anthrax scare that followed the terrorist attack on the US in September 2001, the fear of bio-terrorism has grown massively. It is a much less expensive weapon than nuclear, and cheaper even than chemical weapons, some analysts estimate that the materials for a major biological strike could cost as little as half a million pounds. With its ability to cause both real harm – 30% of all those with smallpox die – and widespread panic, bio-terror is being presented as the choice of attack for the relatively near future.

Tests by American academics of a theoretical smallpox attack showed it could kill around 2,500 people within a fortnight of being introduced into a modern society.

Short of introducing the vaccination of whole populations it is also very hard to protect against such an attack as biological arsenals can be airborne or waterborne, and can spread from person to person by breath or touch. Even vaccination, however, is problematic; there are many different strains of smallpox, for example, with new ones being developed all the time, and a vaccination which protects against one strain may be ineffective against another. The ominous predictions of attacks in London on its Underground system for example, which can be traced all the way to government, show that the fear of a bio-terror attack has become ingrained in the past year or so.

As is the case with chemical weapons, biological warfare has a longer history than might be imagined. Diseased animal carcasses were often hurled into cities during mediaeval sieges, in an attempt to infect the inhabitants, and in the eighteenth century British troops used blankets infected with smallpox as a weapon against Native Americans.

In the twentieth century bio-terror has been developed further through the work of many different governments, including the Japanese, accused of conducting biological warfare experiments on POWs during the Second World War. Cuba, in its long-running dispute with the US has accused America of introducing swine fever into the country that killed 500,000 pigs. The Cubans claim that biological agents have also been sprayed on crops.

Tales of the US military conducting tests within its own country have long been rumoured including a 1966 germ warfare experiment on the New York Subway as well as an outbreak of bacteria in San Francisco.

The anthrax attacks which followed the 11 September attacks in New York which claimed the lives of several people have at least established that the fears are not totally misplaced.

It is still unclear who was responsible for the attacks, with suggestions ranging from bogeymen of the month al-Qaeda, to disaffected US right-wing militias, to a renegade mad scientist.

CHEMICAL TERROR

Britain, Germany, France, Italy, Japan, USA, Indonesia and Iraq. What links these countries and this particular roll of honour? Well, at some stage in their history they have all used chemical weapons as a missile of war. The Soviet Union in Afghanistan and Vietnam in Laos and Cambodia have also been accused, though proof remains sketchy, of doing the same. Yemen also stands accused of using Soviet-supplied chemical weapons. Reports of chemical attacks were made during the Russian Civil War. Aum Shinrikyo (Supreme Truth), the Japanese cult can be added to the list also for their attacks on the Japanese underground in the 1990s.

Chemical attacks, and the increasing fear that their application by a variety of terrorist groups (and countries) is ever more likely, has pushed chemical weaponry to the forefront of the 'War on Terror'.

It is seen as one of the most likely battlefronts of the current 'war'. It is often portrayed as a high-tech development to traditional combat. This is somewhat surprising given its long and established use already in war.

Chemical warfare – the use of gas or chemical agents fired on soldiers and/or civilian populations in the modern age – can be traced back to World War One. The German army, largely through the work of one man, chemist Fritz Haber, was able to develop poisonous gases for use in warfare. Although tear gasses had previously been used by both sides, poison gas was first used on April 22 1915, when at Ypres in Belgium, Germany's officers desperate to break the trench stalemate ordered the release of almost 200 tonnes of chlorine gas on Allied troops.

A thick green fog soon settled around Allied lines. Within two days 5,000 soldiers were dead; 10,000 more were injured many of them with permanent disabilities. Further attacks followed; realising the effectiveness of such deadly assaults the Allies responded in kind.

September 25, 1915 was the date of the first ever chemical attack by Britain. It may not surprise some that the chlorine attack was partly bungled with some of the gas blowing back onto Allied troops.

As a weapon chemical warfare was immediately seen as massively effective.

By 1918, poison gas was estimated to have killed 100,000 soldiers and injured a million. Over 110,000 tonnes of chemical weapons were used during the war. (Haber, who described chemical gas attacks as 'a higher form of killing' went on to collect a Nobel Prize in chemistry then set about developing 'Zyklon B' which the Nazis used in concentration camps in World War Two. Haber, although he renounced his religion, had a Jewish background).

Regulation of chemical weapons began in the 1920s by countries aghast at the brutality of using such arsenals.

In 1925, the Geneva Protocol was signed by 38 countries of the League of Nations prohibiting chemicals for use in war. However, in the same period the Japanese Army used chemical weapons in China and Italians in Abyssinia (Ethiopia).

Britain also used chemical weapons against Kurds seeking independence, Winston Churchill backing their use against 'uncivilised tribes'.

Chemical weapons were not used during World War Two despite considerable stockpiling of gases by the Nazis, who were reckoned to have enough to kill off the entire population of London. (One theory has it that as a soldier in the First World War, Hitler was gassed and refused to use them himself when a leader. Retaliation from the Allies probably played on his mind also).

Production of chemical weapons accelerated after 1945 with the US developing a huge arsenal of weapons.

In fact, the US was the next country that was to use chemical weaponry – and in large measures.

In its defeat in Vietnam it came up with six different herbicides to deforest South Vietnam, the most well-known of these being 'Agent Orange'.

So much was dropped that over 5 per cent of South Vietnam's agricultural cropland was lost, an area which could have been farmed to feed 600,000 people a year.

Agent Orange was linked to a large number of birth defects among the Vietnamese population. In the US in 1968 the amount of herbicides used in Vietnam led to a domestic shortage of household weedkillers.

The US also used CS gas – a virulent tear gas that also burned the skin – in Vietnam, and stored VX at its bases in Japan without informing the Tokyo government. In 1975, the US eventually signed the Geneva Protocol.

The most notable use of chemical weapons after that was by one Saddam Hussein in the Iran-Iraq war in the 1980s. Poison gas is largely thought to have been a contributing factor in Iraq's ultimate – and decidedly Pyrrhic – victory. Though as Saddam was one of the West's best friends at this time it might be worth asking where he got these weapons.

Thousands were killed by Saddam in 1988 in the Kurdish town of Halabjah, one of the crimes for which the Iraqi leader is now being prosecuted by the United Nations, and one which is brought up by US and British political leaders as evidence of the need for 'regime change' in Iraq. It is interesting to note, however, that at the time the US refused to break off relations with Iraq and President Reagan blocked possible sanctions against Iraq.

Fears that the Iraqi leader would again use chemical weapons in the 1991 Gulf War, either against allied troops or as part of the Scud attacks on Israel never materialised.

The chemical weapons threat that exists now centres around the proposition more of these type of weapons are more readily available, with the break-up of the USSR despite attempts to regulate the massive stockpiles accumulated by the Red Army when the country collapsed in 1991.

These can be accumulated by 'rogue states' to be used for their own use or, as current thinking in Washington and London goes, supplied to terror groups.

The large number of scientists out of work since the collapse of the USSR makes the chance of rogue states getting hold of or developing, chemical material much easier according to this thinking.

According to a United Nations report from 1969, chemical warfare agents are "chemical substances, whether gaseous, liquid, or solid, which might be employed because of their direct toxic effects on man, animals and plants". The Chemical Weapons Convention defines toxic chemical weapons as "any chemical which, through its chemical effect on living processes, may cause death, temporary loss of performance, or permanent injury to people and animals."

Many chemical warfare agents are highly toxic and may persist in the environment for long periods of time. The persistence of these agents depends on humidity, temperature, chemical state, and the type of soil and vegetation in the area. There are a number of ways in which chemical warfare agents can affect humans, depending on the agent, and these are via the skin (dermal), inhalation, ingestion of contaminated water or food, or entry through other mucous-lined areas such as the eyes, nose, and open cuts. This section provides a brief description of the four major types of chemical warfare agents and their effects on human health.

THE CHEMICALS AND THEIR EFFECTS

1 Nerve agents: These include agents such as VX, of which Iraq allegedly holds large stockpiles, and Sarin, used by Japanese cult Aum Shiryko in their 1995 attack on the Tokyo underground. Developed from the organophosphate group of insecticides, nerve agents act – perhaps unsurprisingly – on the nervous system, destroying the enzymes used in transmission of nerve impulses to the muscles.

2 Blister agents: The mustard gas – dichlorethylsulphide – used in the First World War was of this type. They act by blistering the skin and mucus membranes, such as the eyes, causing blindness. They can also cause severe bleeding from the lungs if inhaled in quantity.

3 Blood agents: Hydrogen cyanide is a typical blood agent. These act by interfering with the absorption of oxygen into the bloodstream, causing respiratory problems, seizures, and ultimately cardiac arrest.

4 Pulmonary agents: These are liquids dispersed in a gaseous form, and include carbonyl chloride, or phosgene, a gas used by the Germans in the First World War, and work by attacking the lungs. One of their more unpleasant characteristics is that they can have a delayed effect, causing problems up to 48 hours after inhalation.

CYBER-TERRORISM

Moving to another 'future' threat, cyber-terrorism sounds high-tech and futuristic and threatens to be the 'new black' when it comes to terrorist threats. It involves terrorists hacking into a computer terminal to wreak havoc in a variety of ways. It could be to try and bring down the computer system of a major government department, military installation or civic office. The effect could be financial – any repairs or attempts to get a system back up and running could ultimately cost a staggering amount of money as has happened in recent times, with the US seeking the extradition from Britain of a man suspected of such activity.

But cyber-terrorism could also be more deadly. One possible scenario is for the terrorist to hack into the computers that control say, the water supply of a major conurbation and open and close valves to contaminate the water supply with chemicals, even sewage, and then release it. A particularly dastardly terrorist would also have hacked into the computer mainframe of the emergency services or shut down the telephone network to create extra confusion and maximum damage. It all sounds horribly frightening and even worse, plausible. In a modern age when many things are connected to the internet why wouldn't a terrorist look at extending the war by adopting such tactics? In July of 2002 the FBI issued a warning saying that America's water utilities were a target. It claimed that it had found documents in Afghanistan that indicated al-Qaeda was investigating ways of disrupting the American water supply. The only problem is that the American government has put out so many warnings since 11 September that it has become hard to work out which ones have any substance and which ones are little short of nonsense. (An earlier government warning about scuba-diving terrorists seems to fall into this latter category).

However there has been concern in the States for years that its infrastructure is especially vulnerable to attack. This not only concerns the water industry but power networks such as the electricity grid and oil lines. If such an attack could be carried out there seems little doubt that it would have devastating potential. An outbreak of a waterborne disease in 1993 in Milwaukee caused up to 100 deaths and 400,000 illnesses. If an attack were deliberate the devastation could be much more widespread. There are 168,000 separate public water systems in the United States, a vast number to try and protect. New York City has taken the potential threat so seriously that it has upped the daily number of samples it takes to test the quality of its drinking water. How likely it all is though is highly questionable. Can a computer mouse really be more deadly than a bomb? Such an attack would take years to prepare – not necessarily a deterrent to a terrorist group – but it could also prove highly expensive to carry out. Again, that might not be a problem in itself but if as a terrorist you are looking to plan an attack that causes maximum damage at minimum cost, cyberterrorism on anything more than an irritating economic scale may remain a theory, thankfully, rather than an actuality.

Of course, all the talk of al-Qaeda tends to obscure the fact that not all terrorists are part of this rather loose coalition. The real IRA are not al-Qaeda and neither are ETA. In fact, just six months before the 11 September attacks the FBI announced its list of most deadly domestic terrorist groups; at number one was not some renegade army from Montana with a chip on its shoulder about Washington. Instead the Earth Liberation Front (ELF) was placed at the top of the list. Dismissed as misguided idealists by the Wall Street Journal the ELF have managed to do around £25 million worth of damage in the past few years as part of their 'terror' campaign. Initially dismissed as typical of a fringe group, the ELF is now finding more prominence and as the FBI has pointed out has appeared on the political radar of those in power. Chances are it will be registering even more in the future, although its sabotage of capitalism seems positively cuddly compared to the methods of some groups.

Eco-terrorism has essentially grown from the anti-capitalist, Green protest groups that first emerged three decades ago and encouraged by the 'monkey-wrenching' philosophy of Edward Abbey. Eco-terrorist concerns are roughly the same as Green groups but the methods are different. Eco-terrorist groups not only campaign for greater protection of the existing environment but actively campaign for the re-creation of ecological areas for new wild spaces. 'To begin with, we do not believe that it is enough to preserve some of our remaining wilderness. We need to preserve it all, and it is time to recreate vast areas of wilderness in all the planet's ecosystems: identify key areas, close roads, remove developments, and reintroduce wildlife' says the Earth First! website. Eco-terrorist attacks so far have tended to concentrate on the destruction of power lines, the bombing of logging trucks, and the destruction of research concerned with industries such as genetically modified crops.

Eco-warriors portray governments and multi-nationals as the real terrorists for their pursuance of policies that are harmful to the environment; the eco-terrorism is perpetrated to defend all life – in other words it is 'counter-terrorism'. Eco-terrorists have traditionally been non-violent, and their actions have been targeted at pipelines but not people. However, that could be about to change. The ELF recently posted on its website the following statement:

While innocent life will never be harmed in any action we undertake, where it is necessary, we will no longer hesitate to pick up the gun to implement justice, and provide the needed protection for our planet that decades of legal battles, pleading, protest, and economic sabotage have failed so drastically to achieve. We will stand up and fight for our lives against this iniquitous civilization until its reign of terror is forced to an end – by any means necessary. In defence of all life.

The potential for eco-terrorism to grow as a recognized form of direct action is likely to increase as humans take ever more resources from a finite planet. Existing groups have shown their potential and intent to inflict economic damage. The likelihood, as some animal liberation groups or hunt saboteurs have begun to show, is that more eco-warriors will see, in the future, 'no option' but to use violence against those they perceive as doing violence to the planet.

SO, WHERE DO WE GO FROM HERE?

'No one can terrorize a whole nation, unless we are all his accomplices.'

Ed Murrow

The perceived threat of terror is omnipresent and whether the real risk to our safety is more than marginally increased may matter less than the public anxiety which is engendered. Certainly the attacks of 11 September were so shocking – beyond what many of us ever thought imaginable – that now nothing seems too incomprehensible when the potential of an attack is discussed. If that can happen – straight out of a Hollywood plot but real – what is there which would surprise us now? Probably very little and so we have apocalyptic-type warnings from our leaders to beware of suicide attacks on major city centres; to be vigilant in case terrorists target major utilities; or they somehow buy chemical weapons over the internet. Or that they are able to get nuclear weaponry. It is the kind of thing that seemingly belongs in science fiction – and bad science fiction at that, a lame storyline that could easily have been lifted from any 1950s B-film.

It truly is a strange time. And if we were to wake up tomorrow and read about a terrorist outrage we will be appalled, saddened and horrified. However, we probably would not be surprised. That probably says as much as can be said about the period we are all currently living through. Of course, the big question is whether our fears match up to the reality. What will happen as opposed to what could happen? The latest intelligence seems to suggest that attacks on the scale of 11 September remain out of reach of terrorist groups, yet at the same time, governments warn us to prepare for the unimaginable. Could governments in the West be deliberately talking up the threat of terror to justify its actions elsewhere on the globe? Certainly it is not beyond governments to act in such a way. Mark Thomas, in responding to November 2002 alleged threats to release poison gas on the London underground, suggested the evidence for the existence of the plot was less substantial than that existing for the tooth fairy. His point being that the threat is being used to justify other domestic and international policy. Ninety per cent of his readers thought the same in an internet poll.

He and they may have a point, but it *is* also likely that further terrorist outrages will take place. In large part that is because the political and economic victims of the current system cannot see a realistic chance that they will ever be anything other than victims. The current trajectory in global politics seems to be towards further violence and the 'globalization' of small arms. A pessimistic future may involve private armies enforcing the wishes of big companies for instance. So the rhetoric of capitalist democracy – which suggests an optimistic future – flies in the face of its consequences, which are perhaps more stark. Thus the threat of terror hangs desperately close over the heads of all of us every day. But the most obvious potential victims are not necessarily you or me. They are ordinary Iraqis, Palestinians and Colombians and the terror they will face will be much larger than anything that could be unleashed by a single terrorist group, however long it took to plan the attack.

7 SOME CONCLUSIONS ON TERRORISM

'In the battle between good and evil it is the people who get killed'

Eduardo Galeano (*New Statesman*, 2.12.02)

IT MAY HAVE BEEN Salman Rushdie, in fact it probably was, who said that hell must be somewhere where you can only read things you agree with. We know that not all readers of this book will accept all of our arguments, but we hope that it is a feature of democratic society that such arguments can be made. We also hope that the very first paragraph of the book makes it clear that these arguments can still be made by people directly affected by terrorism.

In fact, those even more directly affected can feel the same. In John Pilger's remarkable film 'Palestine is Still the Issue' (a film for which he – surely perversely – received death threats from people protesting against his alleged support of terrorists) a father speaks of the death of his daughter due to a suicide bombing. On 4 September 1997, his 14-year-old daughter, Smadar, was killed by a suicide bomber while shopping with two friends, one of whom was killed, the other seriously injured in the attack. Rami Elhanen is remarkably rational in his response to Pilger years after the attack, but not devoid of emotion: 'I'm not crazy. I don't forget,' he says. 'I don't forgive. Someone who murders little girls, anyone who murders little girls, is a criminal and should be punished.' And of course he is right; it is indisputable. 'But,' he continues, 'if you think from the head and not from the gut, and you look what made people do what they do – people that don't have hope, people who are desperate enough to commit suicide, you have to ask yourself have you contributed in any way for this despair? For this craziness? It hasn't come out of the blue: the boy whose mother was humiliated, in the morning, at the checkpoint, will commit suicide in the evening. The suicide bomber was a victim – the same as my girl was. Of that I am sure.' If such a gentleman can conclude that: 'You have to understand where these suicide bombers come from. Understanding is part of the way to solving the problem' then is a knee-jerk response to terrorism justified?

As has been argued 'to demand understanding of the grievances that give rise to terrorism is not at all the same thing as to demand understanding of the terrorists themselves, still less to excuse their actions.' Knee-jerk reactions cannot work in this case and understanding has to prelude any workable solution; 'Al-Qaeda cannot be engaged as the Wehrmacht was; the west can disrupt terrorist bases, but the effect, as Bali shows, can only be temporary.' (New Statesman, Leader, 21 October 2002). What we need to do is convince the millions of poor throughout the world that a seemingly uncaring West has more answers to their earthly problems than a merciful God and that theocratic fascism is not the answer, because in many parts of the world the idea of 'eternal paradise' seems a good deal more realistic than eternal prosperity to people whose lives are characterized by despair and destitution. But any analysis of cause and effect has been rejected by a simple minded president and hawkish ideologues who surround him. A simple mind may have worked – fortuitously – in the Cold War, but it is not what is needed now. The more bellicose Western leaders become, the more they put us in danger.

Whatever our horror at recent terrorism – quite rightly shared by many people, simple minded and all – we can be helped to move to understanding through analysis of history which gives us distance from events, hence dispassion and insight. We can all dispassionately discuss the unspeakable terror of the French Revolution. It does not threaten our friends and our way of life. We are connected to it only by multiple, mostly untraceable, generations. But you may argue 'the war on terror' is here and now. It has killed people we know or friends of people we know. It has affected places we've been and places we'd like to visit. We don't know that we won't be the next victim of something so mindlessly awful that we cannot comprehend it. In fact when the Bali bombing has just taken place, isn't this liberal 'let's think about it' approach just plain offensive?

We certainly hope not. It is not intended to be. The thought of a Taliban-style regime, for instance, becoming globalized is frankly appalling. But since it is so appalling, from where does such an idea gain recruits? Who would be so, let us say foolish, to die for such a corrupt, unjust society? We think the answer lies near to home. It has been documented in the past that widespread poverty has been a breeding ground for extreme left-wing doctrines, as for instance in the shape of Peru's Sendero Luminoso (Shining Path). Similarly, a down-trodden nation, or nation in decline has frequently promoted extreme nationalist politics, as in the case of Hitler's Germany. What then might promote the adherence in similar fanatical fashion to militant or radical Islam? Well, apart from the Western role in encouraging Arab anti-Semitism in previous centuries, put simply, the coldness of capitalism, the arrogance of America, and the mindless misery of the masses, excluded from Western affluence and excess. In an era of television and travel, the have-nots easily see what the haves enjoy and can lash out at virtually any time or place. Of course not everyone lashes out in this way, but the current ordering of global society encourages extremists; it encourages extreme responses. On human development indexes of the United Nations, roughly speaking an estimate of quality of life, US allies like Saudi Arabia are so unequal and unjust that they finish below Cuba, a nation strangled by US economic blockade for over 40 years. Is it any wonder that for some the rational response is that there must be a better way and that they have literally nothing to lose? Or that so many nations have to keep radical forces controlled by fear?

It is said that in war we become like our enemies. In order to defeat evil we have no choice but to descend ourselves into behaviour which contravenes our deepest moral sentiments. It is them or us. Of course the 'war on terrorism' is not a real war, in the sense that there are no armies with positions, moving frontlines and so on. As Susan Sontag has pointed out, the 'war on terrorism' is a metaphor. It is a rhetorical device designed to create in us a sense of urgency and vigilance. But if we take seriously the idea that war makes us become like our enemies, is this a danger in the war on terror? Let us start answering this by asking what it is, in fact, that characterizes a terrorist.

A terrorist can be said to exhibit a fundamental disregard for human life and a belief that innocent people can be worth sacrificing. This lack of humanity and compassion stems from a belief that means can be justified according to the ends. In other words, terrorists believe totally in their cause to the extent that in order to achieve it no other evil should be allowed to stand in the way. In this sense however the cause may be anti-capitalist, anti- or pro-Christian, anti- or pro-government and so on. In effect the terrorist reserves the right to decide who is worthy or not and who might be killed in the name of the cause. The 'cause' is thus everything and you can be only firmly behind it or against. Those who accept the cause may have total loyalty demanded of them. Terrorist groups are not big on self-criticism, and are remarkably suspicious of others and even their own members.

In some senses then it appears that the war on terrorism is making us all more like our enemies. Criticism and dissent are shouted down or declared disloyal because, according to those directing the war, you can only be for, or against, us. Those under suspicion have been locked up and actions taken covertly which transgress normal rules of behaviour for governments. We are suspicious and intolerant. We demand blood. This last point is key: the war on terrorism seems implicitly to assume that certain groups of people may have to be sacrificed in order for our cause to prevail rather than winning through force of example or argument. And whilst it is possible to make the argument that high-level bombing does not deliberately target innocent civilians, this is only in the sense that a blind-folded man firing a machine gun in a full football stadium cannot be said to be targeting anyone.

Furthermore, in order to hold back waves of sympathy for ideas which breed in destitution and despair, Western governments are also frequently relying on dictatorships and autocracies to clamp down heavily on their own populations and terrorist cells. In encouraging this behaviour, the west is also compelled to turn a blind eye to the human rights abuses which might need to be used in keeping the fundamentalists at bay. But this is, in turn, so much more grist for the mill of the terrorist. Western, often material support, another reason for resentment.

If the war on terrorism means we simply fight evil with evil then it is doomed to failure. We begin to create in global society an expectation of violence. As violence becomes the norm, and normalized, society is degraded. If our societies become more secretive, more suspicious, then our democracy will function less well. And if democratic means of expression are replaced by top-down diktat then we create societies where terrorism becomes one of the few means of expression for excluded people.

Of course we might be wrong in this assessment. In 1932 in El Salvador, General Martinez presided over what has become known as the *Matanza* or massacre. In the space of 2 days in the west of the country perhaps as many as 40,000 (maybe 'only' 10,000) mainly indigenous peoples were slaughtered. The trauma inflicted upon survivors was such that traditional costumes quickly faded from the scene and protest was particularly low. When civil war broke out in El Salvador in the late 1970s, almost 50 years after the *Matanza* it was markedly better supported in east and central El Salvador than the west. So perhaps the war on terrorism could be won if it simply killed many more people, seeking the elimination of cultural difference and the production of a human society based primarily on fear. It sounds like the start of Hollywood future/sci-fi. It seems like some people actually want it to happen. At that point we would need to remind ourselves what we were fighting about in the first place. Given that states have killed 2.5 million people since 1965 (many of these states US allies) and terrorists several thousand, how many people would need to die to wipe out terror in this scenario?

Another potential argument is that we are, at base, animals. Though we can learn, we also have a human nature which conditions responses in a way which is remarkably consistent across the globe. Does our nature make violence inevitable? If it does then perhaps the current situation really does require us to kill or be killed. But though we are animals, we are also a very special animal with the capacity to make moral judgments and exhibit rationality. We can, like robots in science fiction, exceed our programming. We need to recognize that the world is unequal, unfair and unjust. Whilst policies continue to ignore this fact, or whilst we advocate doing the things which keep the rich richer as the solution, some people will always find the sad desperation to commit terrorist acts. The uncomfortable truth is not as uncomfortable as life for the majority.

AFTERWORD

THIS BOOK STARTED with reflections on a friend lost and by the time it has ended a friend of a friend was also killed in Bali. If that then makes me a target of terrorism by association it should be emphasized vehemently that understanding mindlessness in no way condones it. These people are evil. But the other side of the coin 'we are good' used in the immediate aftermath of 11 September by George W. Bush fails to hold true. 'We' have done terrible things too and we have provoked evil. The solution cannot be to fight evil by doing evil and we cannot fight 'perpetual war for perpetual peace.' (Gore Vidal, 2002). The future is surely bleak if we do.

If we accept, as was argued earlier, that terrorism – since it was not used until the French Revolution – emerges along with a discourse of rights (and demands in relation to those rights – particularly democracy), one way to win a war on terror is presumably to create a society where rights are greatly restricted and where demands are met with an iron fist. British Conservative politician Iain Duncan Smith argued in February 2003 that security was much more important than mere compliance with international law and basic human rights. Is this how to win the war? Reducing the rights of those living in free societies? It seems it is part of the solution being offered.

Furthermore, as we have also seen, in the 19th Century *actual* – but limited – terrorist threats were used to justify otherwise unjustifiable actions of the security forces, including censorship, arbitrary arrest and so forth. Thus was the right atmosphere of fear amongst the public ensured, so that these actions were legitimate even if they were nothing do with terrorism. Is this happening now? Well again it certainly seems to be part of the solution.

Another way of combating 'terrorism' is through oppression. In parts of El Salvador we have examples of areas where a people were so totally and brutally oppressed that the collective trauma caused them to accept their fate – not even fighting back 50 years later when the rest of the country was involved in civil war. Is that then how we are trying to win the war against terrorism – through repression of all possible dissent? It might certainly look that way to an Afghani, or even more so to a Palestinian or Iraqi.

In sum, the war on terrorism seems to be about fewer rights, manipulation of the media, repression and a non-recognition of our own brutality. As the Tsarist authorities were unable to prevent change in Russia because they did not recognize reasons for the terror of Narodnaya Volya in the first place, can a war on terrorism win if it does not start with reasons? Do we want preventative or curative medicine? What happens if we 'treat' only the symptoms?

Here it is difficult not to agree with Noam Chomsky; the US could substantially eliminate terrorism in the world tomorrow – it simply needs to stop engaging in it.

Stopping terrorist attacks on the US as President, says William Blum in his book *Rogue State* would take just 3 days.

He says first he will apologize to all the bereaved, the impoverished – all the victims of US imperialism. Then he would tell Israel it was no longer the 51st state, (but oddly enough a foreign country) and announce to the world that US global interventions have come to an end. Finally, he would then reduce the military budget by 90% and pay reparations to US victims. He concludes by saying that that is what he would do on his first three days in the White House, and that on the fourth day he'd be assassinated!

But aside from the political problems of confronting the kind of entrenched power which would assassinate such a President, things cannot change overnight. We have to deal with the situation as it is. And so for all the USA could do, someone might respond to my observations by suggesting that this is a war of good against evil and that terrorism will not be defeated by good intentions but by the *forces* of good. But can we argue we are on the side of good? States have been responsible for so many more deaths than so called terrorists; so many more evil acts, even in the 1990s when there was no longer the over-used and dubious excuse of Soviet sponsored terrorism used by Ronald Reagan.

To say that 'we' are 'good' in this fight amounts to the king claiming that his oppression is 'good' because it has divine sanction. There appears to be no moral basis for it. If the war on terrorism really is about the perpetual struggle between good and evil then it'll be a tricky one. And if we believe that the existence of evil makes force inevitable in human relations that makes it trickier. But the causes of terrorism are currently to be found not just in the evil within each of us, and solutions not just in the goodness either. The causes are in the multiple evils of world politics; until these are addressed by those with the power to do so, until a lot more good is done, terrorism remains certain.

FURTHER READING AND REFERENCES

Antonius, G. (1938), *The Arab Awakening: The Story of the Arab National Movement,* London

Blum, W. (2001), *Rogue State: A Guide to the World's Only Superpower,* London: Zed

Chomsky, N. (1985), *Turning the Tide: US Intervention in Central America and the Struggle for Peace,* London: Pluto Press

Combs, C. (1997), *Terrorism in the Twenty-First Century,* New Jersey: Prentice Hall

Galbraith, J.K. (1992), *The Culture of Contentment,* Boston: Houghton Mifflin Co

Guyatt, N. (2000), *Another American Century: The United States and the World After 2000,* London: Zed

Hertsgaard, M. (2002), *The Eagle's Shadow. Why America Fascinates and Infuriates the World,* London: Bloomsbury

Hoffman, B. (1998), *Inside Terrorism,* London: Victor Gollancz

Hopple, G.W. and Steiner, M. (1984), *The Causal Beliefs of Terrorists: Empirical Results,* McLean VA: Defense Systems

Howard, L. (1992), *Terrorism: Roots, Impact, Responses,* New York: Praeger

Jenkins, B.M. (1980), *The Study of Terrorism: Definitional*

Problems, Santa Monica: Rand Corporation

Karmon, E. (1998) *Intelligence and the Challenge of Terrorism in the 21st Century*

Kelley, K.J. (1988), *The Longest War: Northern Ireland and the IRA*, London: Zed

Laqueur, W. (ed), (1979), *The Terrorism Reader: A Historical Anthology*, London: Wildwood House

Laqueur, W. (1987), *The Age of Terrorism*, New York: Little Brown

The New Statesman. Magazine used as indicated in the text.

Ovendale, R. (1992), *The Origins of the Arab-Israeli Wars* (2nd Edition), Harlow: Longman

Reich, W. (ed), (1990), *Origins of Terrorism: Psychologies, Ideologies, Theologies, States of Mind*, Cambridge, Woodrow Wilson International Center for Scholars: Cambridge University Press

Scruton, R. (1983), *Dictionary of Political Thought*, London: Macmillan

Stern, G. (1974), 'The Use of Terror as a Political Weapon', *Millennium: Journal of International Studies*, Vol 4, No 3, pp.263–270

Zinn, H. (2002), *Terrorism and War*, Seven Stories Press

INTERNET RESOURCES

BBCi
  www.bbc.co.uk
Chomsky, Noam
  www.zmag.org/chomsky/index.cfm
CIAWorldFactbook
  www.cia.gov/cia/publications/factbook
MediaLens
  www.medialens.org
Monbiot, George
  www.monbiot.com
Nuclear Control Institute
  www.nci.org
Pilger, John
  http://pilger.carlton.com/print
Zinn,Howard
  www.thirdworldtraveler.com/Zinn/HZinn_page.html
Zmag
  www.zmag.org/

INDEX

INDEX

INDEX